Creative Fun for 2- to 6-Year-Olds

the Little Hands

BiG FUN

Craft Book

by

Judy Press

illustrated by Loretta Trezzo Braren

WILLIAMSON PUBLISHING • CHARLOTTE, VERMONT

Library of Congress
Cataloging-in-Publication Data
Press, Judy, 1944-
    The little hands big fun craft book: creative
fun for 2- to 6-year-olds/Judy Press.
    p. cm. — (A Williamson little hands book; 3)
    Includes index.
    Summary: Presents over seventy-five simple
arts and crafts activities related to holidays,
school, occupations, travel, nature, home, and
friendship.
    ISBN 0-913589-96-9
    1. Handicraft—Juvenile literature. 2.
Creative activities and seatwork—Juvenile
literature. 3. Early childhood education-
Activity programs—Juvenile literature. [1.
Handicraft.]
I. Title. II. Series.
TT160.P782 1995
745.5—dc20   95-17574
                                            CIP
                                            AC

Cover design: Trezzo-Braren Studio
Interior design: Trezzo-Braren Studio
Illustration: Loretta Trezzo Braren
Printing: Capital City Press

Little Hands and *Kids Can!* are trademarks
of Williamson Publishing Company

Williamson Publishing Co.
P.O. Box 185
Charlotte, Vermont 05445
1-800-234-8791

Manufactured in Mexico
10 9 8 7 6 5 4 3 2 1

DEDICATION

*This book is dedicated to the women of 1314:
Nona, Clara, Esther, Lena, and Annie.*

CONTENTS

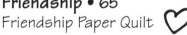

ACKNOWLEDGEMENTS

Having earned a B.F.A. in Art Education from Syracuse University and an M.Ed. in Art Education from the University of Pittsburgh, I would like to acknowledge both schools for their dedication to the arts and to teacher education. I have found teaching art to be immensely satisfying, and I feel privileged to have taught art to many children and adults in the greater Pittsburgh area.

I would like to thank the following for their support and encouragement in the writing of this book: my neighbor Cory Polena, the Mt. Lebanon Public Library, Andrea Perry, Carol Baicker-Mckee, the Children's Book Writing Group of Mt. Lebanon, my husband Allan, and my children Brian, Debbie, Darren, and Matt.

This book would not have been possible without the talent and dedication of the following people at Williamson Publishing: Susan and Jack Williamson, Jennifer Ingersoll, Judy Raven, June Roelle, Jennifer Adkisson, and the creative talent of Ken Braren and Loretta Trezzo Braren.

A WORD TO GROWN-UPS & KIDS

This is a book that celebrates family and friends, national and international holidays, trips and special events. It suggests craft projects, games to play, books to read, gifts to make, and both indoor and outdoor activities. It incorporates a concept of whole learning that will entertain and inform children and grown-ups.

The materials needed to complete the projects in this book are readily available, and the directions are direct and easy to follow. Many of the materials are recycled paper products and packaging materials that would otherwise end up in landfills. Each craft can be embellished in the unique way a child chooses. Have the following supplies on hand before you begin: child safety scissors, white craft glue, tape, package of assorted colors of construction paper, newspaper, shirt cardboard, poster paints in primary colors, a paintbrush, markers, a hole punch, and a stapler.

Craft projects can be created from many of the things we discard, so be an industrious scavenger. Keep a box on hand to save the following: fabric scraps and trim, foil paper, colorful wrapping paper, paper plates and cups, cardboard tubes, Popsicle sticks, dried plant material, seashells, styrofoam trays (from fruits or vegetables only), cardboard boxes, string, and yarn.

As a general rule of safety, always do art in a well-ventilated room, assess your young crafter's propensity to put small objects in his or her mouth (make appropriate materials decisions accordingly), and work with nontoxic materials. Keep in mind that younger siblings may pick up odds and ends from the floor or pull items off the table's edge.

Most items used in these projects can be handled safely by little hands. Where scissors are used, please use child safety scissors — never adult

sharp scissors. It is worth investing in a pair of good child safety scissors that can really cut. Cutting is a skill that children develop slowly, so allow them to practice their cutting skills on scraps of paper and be ready to help if your child is not yet ready to cut with scissors.

Assess your child's readiness when using tools such as staplers and hole punches, too. To prevent any accidents or injuries, very young children should not work directly with these tools. When helping young children, always ask, "Where would you like me to cut?" so the young artist maintains creative control of his or her own project.

When using recycled styrofoam trays, use only those that contained fruits and vegetables. Meat trays, even after washing, may still contain traces of contaminants from uncooked meat. If fruit and vegetable styrofoam trays aren't available to recycle, use a pie tin, piece of cardboard, or heavy paper plate.

Although specific instructions are provided in the book in order to complete a project, remember to allow a child to make choices whenever possible. It is not necessary for crafts to take an exact shape or form; instead encourage new ideas, designs, and individualized interpretations. In a group, each craft should stand out as different from the rest. A grown-up can determine if a younger child may need assistance.

The crafts in this book can be created at special times or for anytime. Memorable times are treasured by each of us, and the sharing of time and space and creative energy are often what children grow to cherish. Through arts, crafts, and celebrations, we can share in the joy of being together in a relaxed atmosphere, where a good time can be had by all who participate. Keep an open mind when crafting with young children, and remember that the experience of creating together is more important than a finished product.

BY ME

EARTH DAY CROWN

Our Earth's a special planet
that spins around the sun,
Keep it clean and treat it well,
it's home to everyone!

HERE'S WHAT YOU NEED

Construction paper (assorted colors including green)

Child safety scissors

White craft glue

Stapler

HERE'S WHAT YOU DO

1 Cut green construction paper 8¾" x 24" (22 cm x 60 cm). Cut long, pointed triangles around paper.

2 Cut flowers, butterflies, trees, fish, sun, clouds, and birds from assorted colors of construction paper. Glue onto points of crown and let dry completely.

3 Wrap crown around head and staple crown edges together.

CUT OUT OBJECTS TO GLUE ON CROWN POINTS

← 8¾" →

24"

CUT OUT CROWN

FIT CROWN ON HEAD AND STAPLE ENDS

MORE BIG FUN!

★ Look closely at the things we throw away. Can you think of a way to use them again?

★ In a box, save things such as seashells, shiny ribbon, pretty paper, old greeting cards, fabric scraps, and yarn. Then, recycle them in art projects.

★ Make a list of things you can do to save the earth. Then, ask your family to help you.

SEWING CARD TREE

We celebrate Arbor Day
as they did years ago,
Planting lots of young new trees
and watching as they grow!

HERE'S WHAT YOU NEED

Shirt cardboard

Hole punch

Markers

Child safety scissors

Yarn

HERE'S WHAT YOU DO

1 Draw the shape of a tree on the cardboard. Cut it out; then punch holes around the tree.

2 Color the tree; then sew through holes with yarn.

WRAP TAPE AROUND END FOR EASY SEWING

MORE BIG FUN!

★ Plant a lemon, orange, or grapefruit seed and watch it grow.

★ Take a nature walk. Learn the name of a tree.

★ Draw a picture of the same tree in winter, spring, summer, and fall.

★ Take some paper and crayons out-doors and do bark rubbings. Does the bark feel *smooth*? *Bumpy*? *Rough*?

★ Look at the leaves on different trees. How do they look *alike*? How are they *different* from each other?

SAWDUST BUGS

When you go out for a walk please take a look around, You'll see creatures in the air, and crawling on the ground!

HERE'S WHAT YOU NEED

2 cups (500 ml) sawdust

1 cup (250 ml) wallpaper paste

Water

Bowl

Pipe cleaner

HERE'S WHAT YOU DO

1 Mix the sawdust and wallpaper paste in the bowl. Slowly add water until a thick dough forms.

2 Shape the dough into sawdust bugs; then poke pieces of pipe cleaner into the heads for antennae. What will you name your bugs?

MIX SAWDUST AND PASTE TOGETHER IN A BOWL; THEN ADD WATER

SHAPE THE THICK DOUGH INTO A BUG

YOU CAN PAINT YOUR BUG WHEN THE DOUGH IS DRY

MORE BIG FUN!

★ Make a whole bug collection — *big ones, little ones, long ones, short ones, fat ones, thin ones, scary ones, and silly ones.*

★ Collect leaves, twigs, acorns, and other natural materials to glue onto cardboard for a nature collage.

★ Place leaves from different trees under thin sheets of paper; then rub a crayon over the tops for leaf rubbings. Staple sheets together for a book about trees.

FANTASTIC FOOTPRINTS

*If you ride a dinosaur,
hold onto its long neck,
And slow it down by shouting,
"Whoa, Tyrannosaurus Rex!"*

HERE'S WHAT YOU NEED

2 styrofoam trays (from fruits or vegetables)

Child safety scissors

Large sheet of paper

Poster paint

Newspaper

HERE'S WHAT YOU DO

 Cover table with newspaper. Pour a small amount of paint into one styrofoam tray.

2 Cut the shape of a dinosaur foot from the other tray; then dip into paint and press down onto paper for dinosaur footprints.

CUT OUT FOOT SHAPE

DIP CUT SHAPE INTO PAINT AND PRESS ONTO PAPER

MORE BIG FUN!

★ Be a print detective! Look for footprints and pawprints in the sand or snow. Can you guess *who* made them? Can you tell from *where* they were coming and where they were going?

★ Dip your feet in water and leave footprints behind on the pavement.

★ Make "pawprints" on steamy windows or mirrors. Press your palm and just the tips of your fingers.

SOCK PUPPET PET

Parakeets, a cockatoo, a turtle, fish, or frog — There are lots of pets to love besides a cat or dog!

HERE'S WHAT YOU NEED

2 old socks

Child safety scissors

White craft glue

Scrap fabric

Rubber bands

HERE'S WHAT YOU DO

 1 Stuff one sock into the other (do not go as far as the toe).

2 Cut the toe down the center, and wind a rubber band around each half of the sock's toe for ears. Wrap another rubber band around the bottom of the stuffing for a neck.

3 Cut a hole on both sides of the sock for fingers.

4 Cut out fabric scraps for the puppet's eyes, mouth, and nose; then glue them onto your puppet pet.

LEAVE ROOM AT TOP TO CUT DOWN CENTER FOR EARS

CUT

STUFF ONE SOCK INTO THE OTHER

CUT OUT ARM HOLE

CUT OUT ARM HOLE

MORE BIG FUN!

★ Make several sock puppet pets and have a puppet show.

★ Cut pictures of animals from old magazines in half. Invent new animals by putting unmatched halves together.

★ Read *Socks For Supper* by Jack Kent.

ARGYLE

★ Name your sock puppet pets. What's a good name for a sock bunny?

FOUR SEASON TREES

When autumn leaves fall from the trees,
they flutter to the ground,
Rake them all up and you will find,
There's always more around!

HERE'S WHAT YOU NEED

2 toilet tissue tubes

4 pieces shirt cardboard

Child safety scissors

Poster paint

Paintbrush

White craft glue

HERE'S WHAT YOU DO

1. Hold the tubes upright; then ask a grown-up to cut them in half vertically. Glue each half onto one shirt cardboard for tree trunks. Let dry completely.

2. Paint the tube tree trunk brown. Paint branches and seasonal leaves on the cardboard or collect leaves outdoors to glue on.

MORE BIG FUN!

★ Press autumn leaves between clear contact paper; then punch a hole in the top and hang from a string.

NOODLE NAME TAG

When the school year starts,
summer draws to an end,
It's a great time
to make a few new friends!

HERE'S WHAT YOU NEED

Alphabet noodles

Shirt cardboard

Poster paint

Small paintbrush

Large safety pin

Child safety scissors

Tape

White craft glue

HERE'S WHAT YOU DO

 1 Cut the cardboard into a 4" x 1" (10 cm x 2.5 cm) rectangle, and paint. Let dry; then tape the safety pin to the back.

2 Use the alphabet noodles to spell your name. Glue them on the front of the cardboard. Let dry completely.

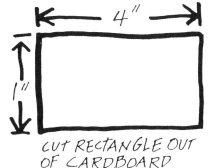

4"

1"

CUT RECTANGLE OUT OF CARDBOARD

TAPE SAFETY PIN TO BACK

JOHN

GLUE NOODLES ON FRONT TO SPELL OUT YOUR NAME. YOU CAN EVEN COLOR THE NOODLES WITH PAINT!

MORE BIG FUN!

★ Use other pasta shapes to spell a name or message on a larger piece of cardboard; then hang from string around a doorknob.

MY ROOM

★ Read *Annabelle Swift, Kindergartner* by Amy Schwartz.

★ Ask a partner to draw letters on your palm with a finger while you close your eyes. Can you guess what the letters are? Take turns drawing and guessing.

A? ?B C?

APPLE PRINT BOOK BAG

*Teachers make a classroom
an exciting place to learn,
"Call me! I know the answer!"
each student shouts in turn.*

HERE'S WHAT YOU NEED

Apple

Plain canvas tote bag or
brown bag with handle
(see page 106)

Fabric paint

Heavy paper plate

Newspaper

Paper towel

HERE'S WHAT YOU DO

1 Cover the table with newspaper. Ask a grown-up to use a knife to cut the apple in half. Pat dry the cut side of the apple.

2 Pour a thin layer of fabric paint into the plate. Dip the flat side of the apple into paint. Press onto bag for apple prints.

CUT

DIP FLAT SIDE OF APPLE INTO PAINT; THEN PRESS DOWN ON BAG

MORE BIG FUN!

★ Use poster paint to print apples on brown paper bags; then wrap your books with printed paper.

★ Talk about your favorite books. What makes them special to you?

★ Try printing with vegetables such as carrots, celery, onions, and potatoes.

★ Make prints on old pillowcases or undershirts.

SANDPAPER LETTER RUBBINGS

The alphabet's many letters
begin with ABC,
They spell big words like "atmosphere"
and little ones like "be"!

HERE'S WHAT YOU NEED

White craft glue

Sheet of sandpaper

Child safety scissors

Cardboard

Thin white paper

Crayons

HERE'S WHAT YOU DO

1 Cut letters from the sandpaper; then glue letters onto cardboard. Let dry completely.

2 Lay thin paper over the sandpaper. Rub crayons back and forth until letters appear.

I O LOV E YU

CUT LETTERS FROM SANDPAPER

GLUE
GLUE LETTERS ON CARDBOARD

LAY THIN PAPER OVER CARDBOARD

RUB CRAYON ON PAPER

MORE BIG FUN!

★ Write your initials with sandpaper letters.

A.T.I.

★ Read Chicka Chicka Boom Boom by Bill Martin.

★ Close your eyes and feel the sandpaper. Can you guess what letter it is?

COLOR MATCH GAME

Red spaghetti, purple peas,
and bright green cookie dough,
If colors are all mixed up,
you'll have a food rainbow!

HERE'S WHAT YOU NEED

Index cards

Crayons

RED

BLUE

HERE'S WHAT YOU DO

 1 Use each crayon to color one side of two index cards.

2 Place cards color-side down, and mix them up. To play the game, turn cards over, two at a time, until a match is made. Continue until all colors are matched.

 3 Play with a friend. (You lose your turn if there is no match.)

COLOR ONE SIDE OF TWO CARDS THE SAME COLOR

MIX UP CARDS, COLOR-SIDE DOWN

MORE BIG FUN!

★ Draw two pictures or shapes that are the same color on two index cards. Turn cards over and play the matching game.

★ Make colored ice cubes by adding food coloring to water before freezing. Watch 2 different colors melt together in a glass.

★ Are your favorite foods all one color — or do you like a "rainbow" of foods?

SPARKLING SHAPES MOBILE

*A shape that's neither square nor round
has a funny name,
It's called an octagon and has
eight sides all the same!*

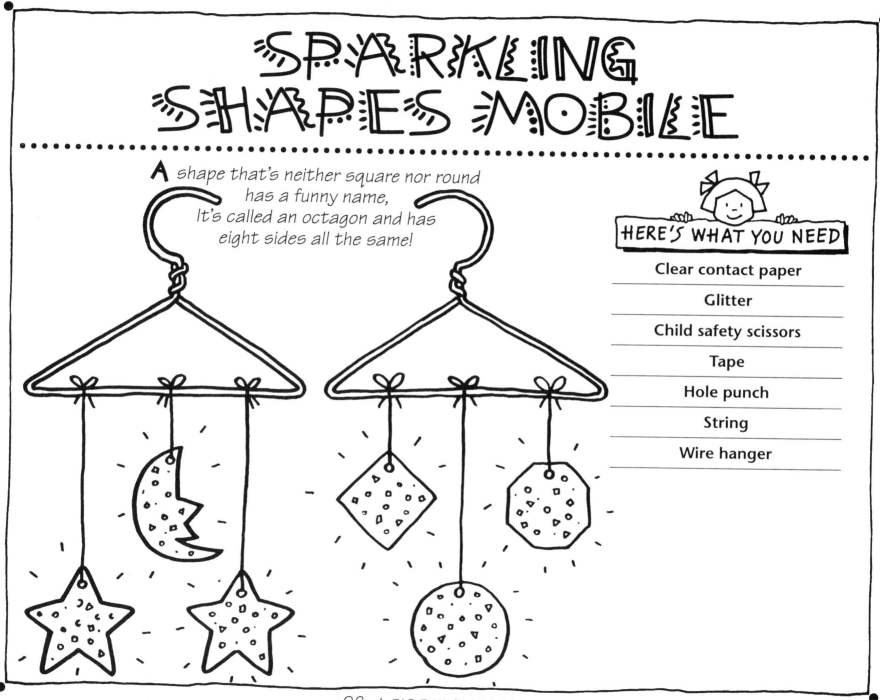

HERE'S WHAT YOU NEED

Clear contact paper

Glitter

Child safety scissors

Tape

Hole punch

String

Wire hanger

HERE'S WHAT YOU DO

 Sprinkle glitter onto sticky side of contact paper. Cover with a second piece of contact paper. Cut the contact paper into shapes.

 Punch a hole in the top of each shape; then thread different lengths of string through each hole.

3 Tie sparkling shapes to the wire hanger with string. Tape to hold in place.

GLITTER

STICKY SIDE

COVER WITH
OTHER SHEET OF CONTACT
PAPER, STICKY-SIDES TOGETHER

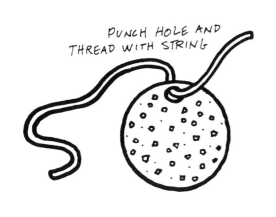

PUNCH HOLE AND
THREAD WITH STRING

CUT OUT SHAPES

MORE BIG FUN!

★ Sprinkle hole punch paper circles or confetti onto contact paper; then cut into shapes and tie to a wire hanger for a mobile.

★ Go on a shape hunt around your home or school. How many *circles* can you find? *Squares*? *Triangles*?

★ Think of some things that sparkle. Look at different kinds of rocks, the stars in the sky, or the surface of the water on a sunny day.

CEREAL COUNTER

It's easy to count toes and the slices in a pie, Much harder to count stars glowing brightly in the sky!

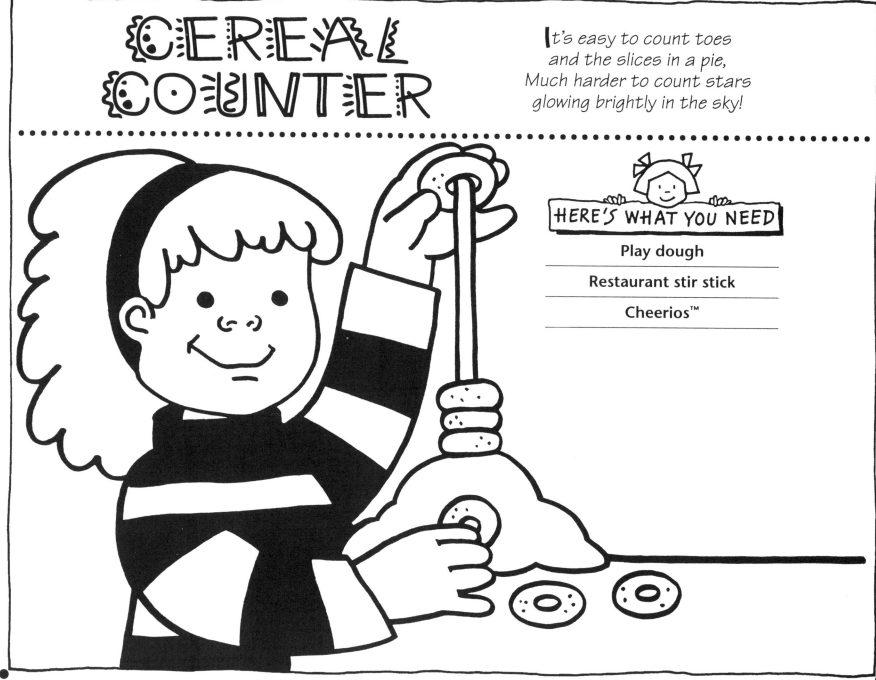

HERE'S WHAT YOU NEED

Play dough

Restaurant stir stick

Cheerios™

HERE'S WHAT YOU DO

1 Stand stir stick upright in play dough.

2 Count each Cheerio™ as it slides down on the stick.

MOLD PLAY DOUGH INTO A BASE

STAND STICK IN CENTER OF PLAY DOUGH BASE

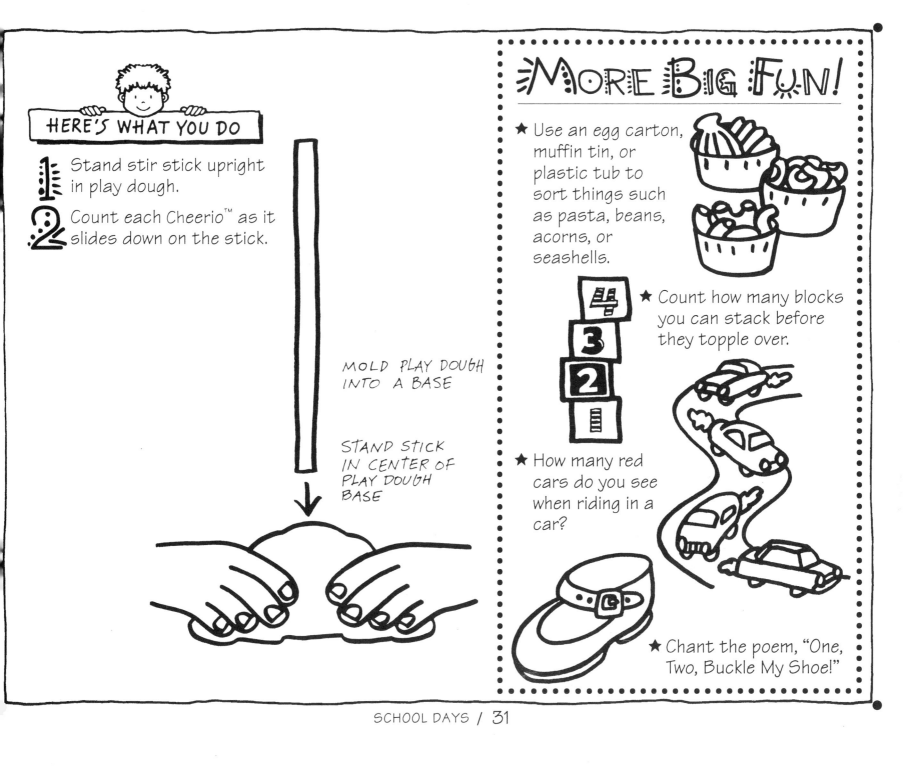

MORE BIG FUN!

★ Use an egg carton, muffin tin, or plastic tub to sort things such as pasta, beans, acorns, or seashells.

★ Count how many blocks you can stack before they topple over.

★ How many red cars do you see when riding in a car?

★ Chant the poem, "One, Two, Buckle My Shoe!"

COOKIE SHEET CLOCK

*Clocks tick away the seconds,
count minutes in the day,
They tell you when it's bedtime,
and when it's time to play!*

HERE'S WHAT YOU NEED

**Styrofoam trays
(from fruits or vegetables)**

Magnetic tape

Marker

Cookie sheet

Child safety scissors

HERE'S WHAT YOU DO

 1 Cut twelve circles and the hands of a clock from styrofoam trays.

 2 Attach a small strip of magnetic tape to the back of each circle and the clock's hands.

3 Write the hour on the circles; then place them onto the cookie sheet for a clock. Point clock's hands to tell time.

CUT CIRCLES AND CLOCK HANDS FROM TRAYS

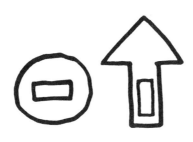

ATTACH MAGNETIC TAPE STRIPS ON BACK OF CIRCLES AND HANDS

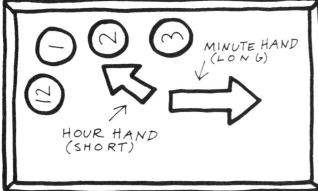

MINUTE HAND
(LONG)

HOUR HAND
(SHORT)

MORE BIG FUN!

★ Move the hands of the clock to tell what time you go to bed. Then, read *Bedtime For Francis* by Russel Hoban.

★ Count how many clocks are in your house. How *many* have digital (print out) numbers? How many have hands?

★ Draw a picture of your favorite time of day.

WEATHER WATCH BOARD

When it's sunny in the morning and then the sky turns grey, It's time to put your slicker on 'cause rain is on the way!

HERE'S WHAT YOU NEED

Felt (assorted colors)

Large shoe box

Sticky-backed Velcro

Child safety scissors

White craft glue

Marker

HERE'S WHAT YOU DO

 1 Trace the shoe box lid onto a large felt scrap; then cut out felt and glue to the top of the lid.

2 Draw weather shapes such as a sun, clouds, umbrella, and a snow-man onto felt. Cut out the shapes; then glue Velcro to their backs.

 3 Look for signs that hint what the weather will be. Place your prediction shape on the Weather Watch Board before you go to bed. Were you right?

ATTACH VELCRO TO BACK OF WEATHER SHAPES

MORE BIG FUN!

★ Use puffy fabric paint to decorate the felt shapes.

★ There are many signs that help us predict what is about to happen. Can you tell when a thunderstorm is near? Are the clouds heavy and dark? Is the dog hiding? Is your neighbor bringing in the laundry? What are the signs of a snowstorm? A very hot day?

★ Draw lines every 1/2" (1 cm) up the side of a clear plastic cup; then place outside and wait for rain. How much rain fell during the storm?

POLKA-DOT LUNCH BAG

Try packing a lunch that's tasty and also good for you, Make sandwiches on whole-grain bread, add fruits and veggies, too!

HERE'S WHAT YOU NEED

Small brown paper bag

Pencil (with eraser)

Poster paint

Heavy paper plate

Newspaper

HERE'S WHAT YOU DO

1 Cover the table with newspaper. Then, pour a thin layer of paint into a heavy paper plate.

2 Dip the eraser into the paint; then press onto bag for polka-dots. Let dry completely before packing lunch.

MORE BIG FUN!

★ Use the eraser to print a name or special message on the lunch bag.

★ Play connect-the-dots on the bag when you're done with lunch.

★ Talk about your favorite foods for lunch. How do they taste? Are they salty like pretzels? Sweet like sugar? Sour like pickles?

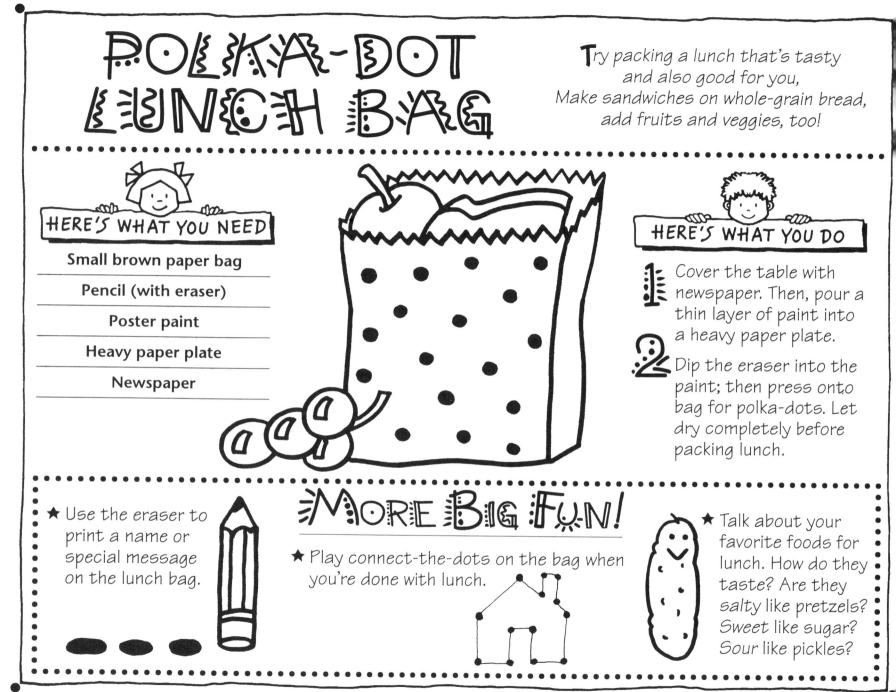

BIG FUN CRAFTS

BOTTLE BOWLING PINS

The bowling ball is headed straight toward the pins, And if every pin falls down, you're the one who wins!

HERE'S WHAT YOU NEED

Large plastic soda bottles

Funnel and clean sand

Stickers

Tennis ball

HERE'S WHAT YOU DO

1 Soak bottles in warm water to remove labels; then use the funnel to fill bottles one-third full of sand. Screw tops back on bottles.

2 Decorate bottles with stickers.

3 Arrange bottles (at least three) for a bowling game. How many pins can you knock down with one ball?

PLACE STICKERS ON BOTTLES FOR DECORATION

POUR SAND INTO BOTTLE THROUGH FUNNEL

PLASTIC SODA BOTTLE →

⅓ MARK

★ Visit a bowling alley. *Listen* to the sounds of the rolling balls and falling pins.

★ Can you pick up a bowling ball? It is very *heavy*. Maybe you can ask to *touch* a ball, to *feel* the chalk dust, and *rub* your hand on the smooth bowling alley. Then, have fun watching someone bowl.

BOBBING BOAT

A boat bobs on the ocean,
and wind fills up the sail,
It could be a rough ride,
so hold on to the rail!

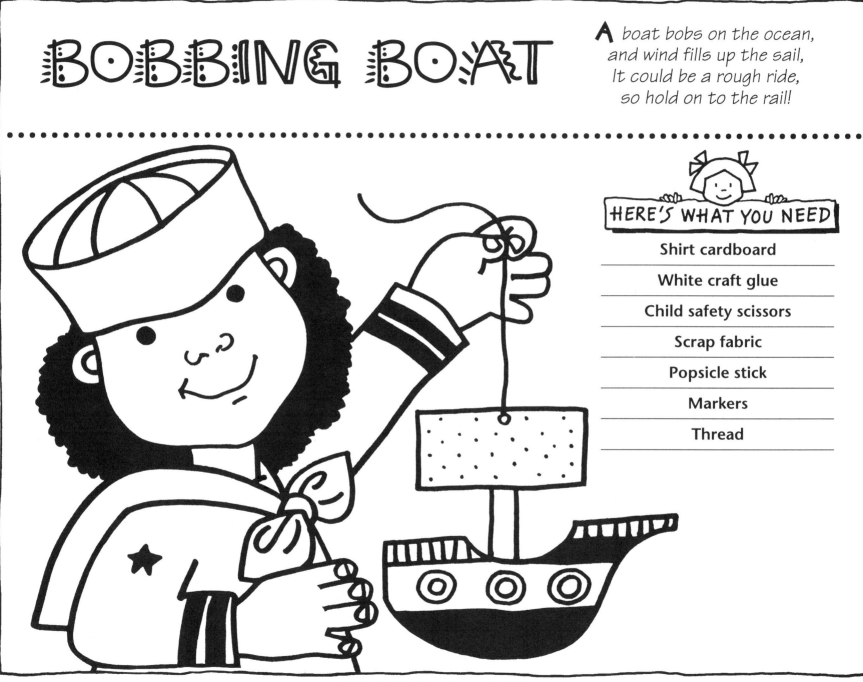

HERE'S WHAT YOU NEED

Shirt cardboard

White craft glue

Child safety scissors

Scrap fabric

Popsicle stick

Markers

Thread

HERE'S WHAT YOU DO

 1 Cut the shape of 2 hulls and 1 sail from shirt cardboard. Decorate the hull with markers.

 2 Trace the cardboard sail twice onto scrap fabric. Cut out and glue fabric on both sides of the sail.

3 Press Popsicle stick between 2 hulls; then glue together. Glue sail on Popsicle stick.

4 Hang boat from thread tied to small hole in sail.

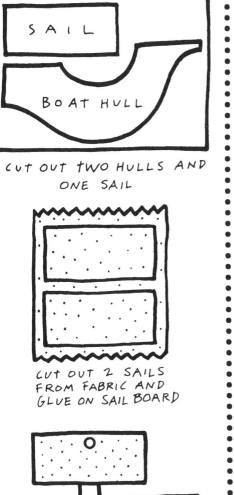

CUT OUT TWO HULLS AND ONE SAIL

CUT OUT 2 SAILS FROM FABRIC AND GLUE ON SAIL BOARD

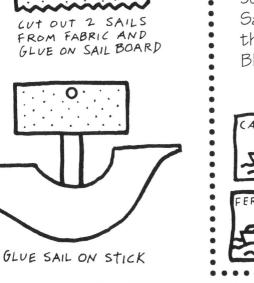

GLUE STICK BETWEEN HULLS

GLUE SAIL ON STICK

MORE BIG FUN!

★ Make a boat mobile. Hang the boats from a branch or wire coat hanger.

★ Glue your boat onto paper and paint the ocean and sky.

★ Sing the song, "Sailing, Sailing, Over the Ocean Blue."

CANOE

FERRY

★ Cut out pictures in magazines of different kinds of boats. Have you ever been on a ferry? A sailboat? A fishing boat? A canoe?

PIE TIN WIND CHIMES

Wind fills the sails on boats; and whistles through the trees, Kites fly high in the sky, and chimes ring in the breeze!

HERE'S WHAT YOU NEED

Empty pie tin

Child safety scissors

String

Pointed tool
(for grown-up use only)

Metal spoons

HERE'S WHAT YOU DO

POKE HOLES AROUND RIM AND CENTER OF PIE TIN

 Turn pie tin upside down. Ask a grown-up to use the pointed tool to poke holes around the rim and in the center of the tin.

 Cut string into different lengths (save a long piece to hang the pie tin). Tie string through holes.

 Wrap string around spoons and hang in an open window or outside.

WRAP DIFFERENT STRING LENGTHS AROUND SPOONS

MORE BIG FUN!

★ String seashells, nails, aluminum can flip-tops, or bottle caps from a pie tin for a wind chime.

★ Staple together a sheet of construction paper to form a long tube. Tie a string around the top to hang the tube; then glue long streamers at the bottom for a wind sock.

★ Listen to the sound the wind makes on a windy day. Do the trees' leaves rustle? Are flags waving? What other signs tell you the wind is blowing?

CARDBOARD CARTON STORAGE CART

Place your books back on the shelf,
put all your toys away,
Make your bed, pick up your clothes,
it must be clean-up day!

HERE'S WHAT YOU NEED

Cardboard box

Shirt cardboard

Child safety scissors

Wrapping paper

Markers and tape

Paper fasteners

White craft glue

HERE'S WHAT YOU DO

REMOVE FLAPS FROM BOX TOP →

1 Cut four 1" (2.5 cm) squares from the lid of the cardboard box. Cut four wheels from shirt cardboard.

2 Wrap box in paper and tape in place. Use markers to decorate cardboard wheels.

3 Glue squares on the outside of the box where the wheels are to be mounted. Poke a hole through the wheels and the squares; then use a fastener to attach decorative wheels on the sides of the box.

CUT OUT 1" SQUARES FROM FLAPS

CUT OUT WHEELS FROM SHIRT CARDBOARD

WRAP BOX IN PAPER

PUSH FASTENER THROUGH HOLES →

POKE HOLES

GLUE SQUARES ON BOX

MORE BIG FUN!

★ Store toys, clothes, puzzle pieces, and games in your cart.

MY TOYS

★ Play a beat-the-clock game: Use an egg timer or stop watch and see how many minutes it takes to clean up your room.

★ Put on your favorite music when doing chores. You can work to the beat, and hum along, too.

PICTURE PUZZLE

*When all is quiet,
you can still have fun,
Whisper while you're playing,
Tiptoe, and don't run!*

HERE'S WHAT YOU NEED

Old magazines

Cardboard

White craft glue

Markers

Child safety scissors

HERE'S WHAT YOU DO

1. Cut out a picture from an old magazine. Glue it onto cardboard and trim the edges.

2. On the back of the cardboard, draw puzzle pieces; then cut out along the lines. Put pieces together for a puzzle. The smaller the pieces, the more difficult the puzzle.

GLUE PICTURE ON CARDBOARD

DRAW PUZZLE PIECES ON BACK OF CARDBOARD

MORE BIG FUN!

★ Glue a drawing or large photograph onto cardboard; then cut out pieces for a puzzle.

★ Play card games, read a book, draw a picture, or put photos in an album during "please-be-quiet" times.

★ Sometimes when people are confused, they are said to be *puzzled*. Have you ever been *puzzled* about something?

CARDBOARD BOX BOOKSHELVES

When you have a question, the answer's in a book, Librarians can help by showing where to look!

HERE'S WHAT YOU NEED

3 cardboard boxes — approx. 10" (25 cm) x 13" (32.5 cm) x 9" (22.5 cm)

Poster paint

Paintbrush

Paper plate

Newspaper

HERE'S WHAT YOU DO

1 Cover table with news-paper; then pour a small amount of paint into the plate. Paint boxes with poster paint; then let dry completely.

2 Stack boxes or place them side-by-side for bookshelves.

POUR PAINT INTO PLATE; THEN PAINT BOX

MORE BIG FUN!

★ Decorate the bookshelf boxes with stickers or sponge paint (see page 96).

★ Visit your library and apply for a library card.

MY LIBRARY CARD 00123

★ Find out if your library has a story hour. A librarian will read many wonderful books to you and your friends.

★ Sort your books by kinds (mysteries, science, stories) or by *author*. Stack them together in your bookcase.

TRAY SAILBOAT

Create a boat from paper,
try making two or three,
Set sail upon the water,
pretend you've gone to sea!

CUT BOAT FROM TRAY

STICK TOOTHPICK IN CENTER

Styrofoam tray
(from fruits or vegetables)

Construction paper

Child safety scissors

Toothpick

Stapler

Markers

Straw

1 Cut the shape of a sailboat from the styrofoam tray. Poke the toothpick in the styrofoam.

2 Cut a sail from construction paper and decorate.

3 Staple the sail onto the straw and slip the straw over the toothpick.

MORE BIG FUN!

★ For a sailing painting, dampen white paper with water. Brush on poster paint for sea and sky. Let dry. Use markers to draw boats on the water.

★ What kind of boats go the fastest? The slowest? Which kind would you use on a pond? On a lake? On the ocean?

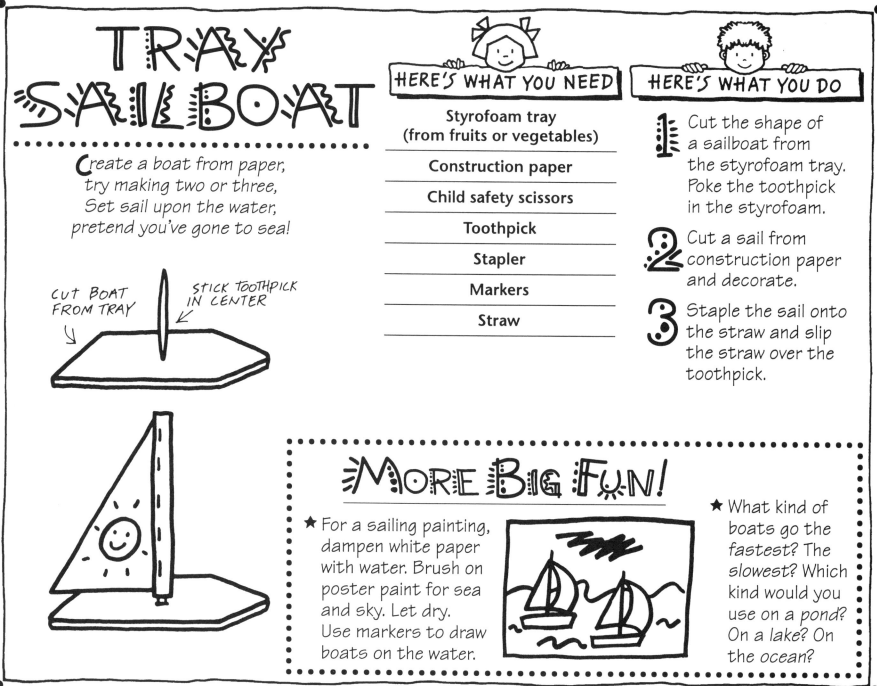

"ALL ABOUT ME" SCRAPBOOK

It's fun to have a scrapbook
of your very own
For looking at the pictures
to see how you've grown!

HERE'S WHAT YOU NEED

Construction paper

White paper

White craft glue

Hole punch

Ribbon or ring binders

Markers

Old family photos

HERE'S WHAT YOU DO

1 Glue white paper onto sheets of construction paper for the book's pages.

2 Punch three holes down the side of each sheet; then put binder rings or ribbon through the holes to hold pages together.

3 Draw with markers, or glue on old photos for a book all about you.

CONSTRUCTION PAPER ↓

WHITE PAPER

USE A HOLE PUNCH TO MAKE THREE HOLES IN EACH SHEET

MORE BIG FUN!

★ Talk to grandparents or other friends about how times have changed since they were children. What kind of transportation did they have? What was the same? Different?

★ Keep a growth chart on your bedroom wall. Ask a grown-up to mark how tall you are on each birthday.

HANDPRINT FAMILY TREE

It's hard to think of grandparents as kids like you or me, Who once enjoyed a game of tag and climbing up a tree!

DAD 8/4/59
MOM 6/9/61
JOE
ANN
ME
PAT

FAMILY TREE

HERE'S WHAT YOU NEED

Roll of shelf paper or butcher paper

Construction paper

Child safety scissors

White craft glue

Paint roller

Marker

Poster paint (brown)

Styrofoam tray (from fruits or vegetables)

HERE'S WHAT YOU DO

1 Pour a thin layer of paint into the tray; then roll paint onto paper for a tree trunk and branches. Let dry completely.

2 Trace hands onto construction paper; then cut them out.

3 Glue paper hands onto tree branches. Write names and birth dates on each paper hand.

ROLL PAINT ONTO PAPER IN THE SHAPE OF A TREE

GLUE CUT OUT PAPER HANDS ON TREE

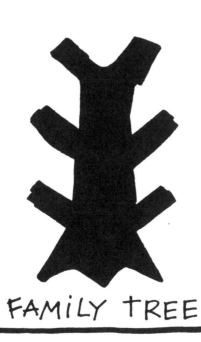

FAMILY TREE

MORE BIG FUN!

★ Press hands in puffy fabric paint; then print on a T-shirt. Use a fabric marker to write names and birth dates.

STEVE
9/1/90

GRANNY AND POPPY

★ Draw a portrait of your grand-parents; then frame it with Popsicle sticks and give it as a gift.

★ Talk about the ways people change as they grow up. Look at a baby picture of you. Have you gotten *taller* since you were a baby? Do you have more hair? How are you *different* from a grown-up?

WE'RE SO PROUD! MEDAL

When someone in the family deserves your admiration, Show how proud you are, with a big celebration!

HERE'S WHAT YOU NEED

Shirt cardboard

String

White craft glue

Child safety scissors

Recycled aluminum foil

Yarn

HERE'S WHAT YOU DO

1 Squeeze glue in a design on a circle cut from the cardboard. Then, press string into the glue. Let dry.

2 Wrap foil around the cardboard. Use your finger to gently press around the string design.

3 Thread yarn through a hole punched in the top of the medal to wear loosely around neck.

SQUEEZE GLUE ON CIRCLE IN A DESIGN

PRESS STRING INTO GLUE

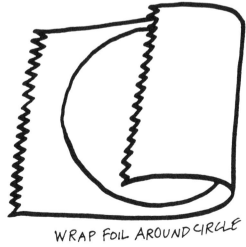

WRAP FOIL AROUND CIRCLE

THREAD YARN THROUGH HOLE

MORE BIG FUN!

★ Plan a special dinner and serve the award winner's favorite food.

★ Cut a band of construction paper 18" wide (45 cm). Measure the length to fit around the head; then cut a zigzag shape into top of the band. Overlap the ends and tape together for an award-winner's crown.

★ Talk about what it means to be proud of yourself or someone else. Who or what are you proud of?

HEARTS & FLOWERS NECKLACE

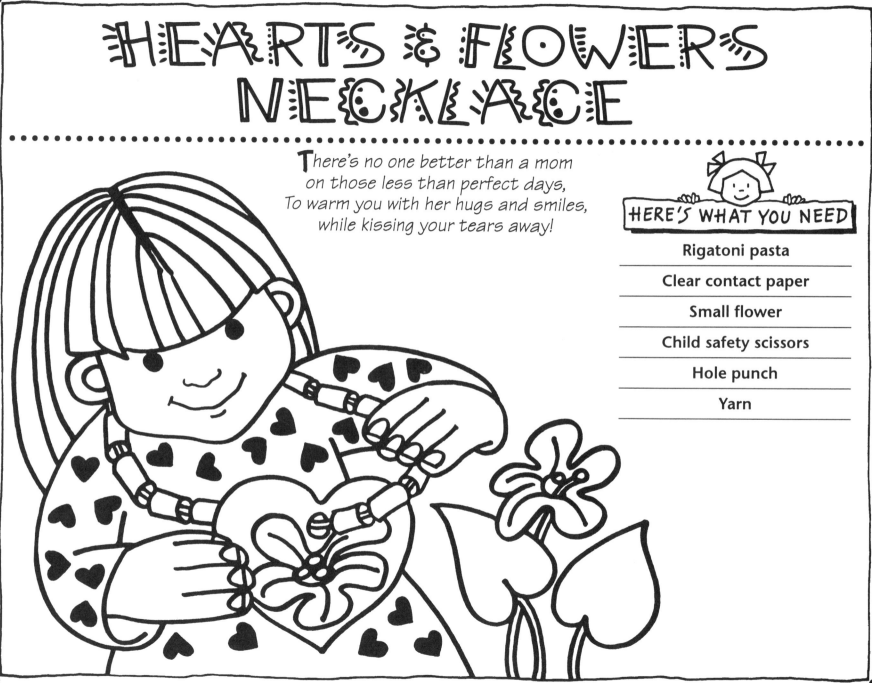

There's no one better than a mom
on those less than perfect days,
To warm you with her hugs and smiles,
while kissing your tears away!

HERE'S WHAT YOU NEED

Rigatoni pasta

Clear contact paper

Small flower

Child safety scissors

Hole punch

Yarn

HERE'S WHAT YOU DO

1 String rigatoni pasta onto yarn.

2 Press the flower between two pieces of contact paper. Cut into a heart shape.

3 Punch hole in top of heart and hang from pasta necklace with yarn.

PRESS FLOWER BETWEEN TWO SHEETS CONTACT PAPER; THEN CUT OUT HEART SHAPE

MORE BIG FUN!

★ Trace handprints onto construction paper; then cut them out. Write a chore or good deed that you are willing to do on each hand. Glue the hands onto Popsicle sticks and push them into a flower-pot for a "helping hand" plant.

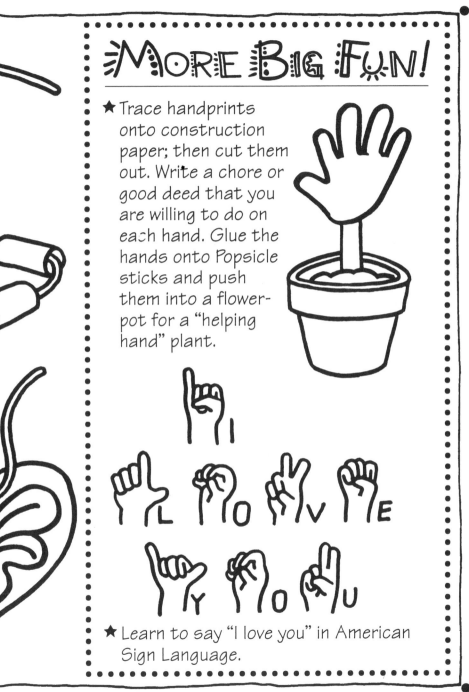

★ Learn to say "I love you" in American Sign Language.

STOCKING FINGER PUPPET

There's something more exciting than T.V. or video,
Watch the curtain going up on your funny puppet show!

HERE'S WHAT YOU NEED

Old nylon stocking

Old white sock

Toilet tissue tube

Scrap fabric

Yarn

Rubber band

Child safety scissors

White craft glue

1. Fold the sock in a ball; then stuff it in the toe of a nylon stocking. Thread stocking through the cardboard tube until puppet's head sock rests on top. Pull excess stocking back up over outside of tube and secure with a rubber band.

2. Use fabric to cover cardboard tube. Glue on scrap fabric for puppet's eyes, nose, and mouth; then glue on yarn for puppet's hair.

SOCK

STOCKING

TUBE

EXCESS STOCKING

COVER TUBE WITH FABRIC

GLUE ON YARN HAIR

GLUE ON EYES, NOSE, AND MOUTH

MORE BIG FUN!

★ Perform a puppet show behind an old sheet hanging between two chairs.

★ Make puppets of everyone in your family. Role-play different situations at home and try to come up with ways of solving problems.

★ Glue on cotton balls for beards, hair, and bushy eyebrows.

COZY KITTY PILLOW

*Find a cozy corner,
then turn on the light,
Pick your favorite story,
read a book tonight!*

HERE'S WHAT YOU NEED

Old pillowcase (solid color)

Round pillow form

Rubber bands

Fabric glue

Fabric paint

Child safety scissors

Yarn (black)

Cardboard

Long ribbon or yarn

HERE'S WHAT YOU DO

 Wrap rubber bands around two corners of the pillowcase for kitten's ears.

 Insert cardboard into pillowcase; then use fabric paint to paint on a kitten's face. Let dry; then remove cardboard and insert the round form.

3 Glue on yarn for whiskers. Tie a ribbon or yarn tightly around the bottom.

FOR EARS, WRAP RUBBER BANDS AROUND CORNERS

INSERT CARDBOARD, PAINT FACE; THEN REMOVE CARDBOARD

INSERT FORM AND GLUE ON YARN WHISKERS; THEN TIE YARN AROUND BOTTOM

MORE BIG FUN!

★ Post a chart in your reading corner to keep track of the books you've read yourself or have had read to you. Next to the chart hang a small pouch for library cards and bookmarks.

★ Invite a friend to share reading time in your cozy corner.

★ Ask a grown-up to read to you before you go to bed each night.

★ Make sound effects to go with your favorite story — growls, thunder, screeches, the wind.

TOOTH FAIRY POUCH

*Don't worry if you've lost a tooth
and have a funny grin,
One day you'll be surprised to see,
another one's grown in!*

HERE'S WHAT YOU NEED

Toilet tissue tube

Scrap fabric and trim

White tissue wrapping paper

Scrap of shirt cardboard

Markers and stapler

Yarn and tape

White craft glue

HERE'S WHAT YOU DO

1 Staple together bottom of the cardboard tube. Wrap fabric around tube and glue in place.

2 Accordion-fold tissue and glue on back of tube for wings. Cut shape of fairy face and neck from cardboard. Draw eyes, nose, and mouth; then tape inside tube. Glue on yarn for hair.

3 Tie yarn to sides of tube and hang pouch from a doorknob or headboard. Glue on fabric trim for decoration.

MORE BIG FUN!

★ Draw a picture of what you look like when you lose a tooth.

FRIENDSHIP

FRIENDSHIP PAPER QUILT

*There was a man with a dream,
named Martin Luther King,
He wished for peace and friendship,
and the love they would bring!*

HERE'S WHAT YOU NEED

Construction paper

Ruler

Child safety scissors

Hole punch

Yarn

Large needle (use with grown-up only)

HERE'S WHAT YOU DO

1 Cut construction paper into 6" by 6" (15 cm x 15 cm) squares. Punch holes around outer edges of the squares.

2 Give paper squares to friends and family. Ask each person to draw a self-portrait.

3 Ask a grown-up to help you thread the needle with yarn and sew squares together for a friendship paper quilt.

PUNCH HOLES AROUND EDGES OF PAPER SQUARE

COLLECT SELF-PORTRAITS OF FAMILY AND FRIENDS

SEW SQUARES TOGETHER WITH YARN THROUGH HOLES ALONG EDGES

MORE BIG FUN!

★ Ask friends, classmates, or neighbors to write a favorite family recipe on an index card. Make photocopies of the recipes; then staple together for a friendship cookbook.

COOKBOOK

★ Are you someone's friend? What does it mean to be a friend?

★ Read *A Picture Book of Martin Luther King Jr.* by David A. Adler.

LOVE PLANTS

Is there someone very special,
to give a valentine?
Sign your name with plenty of love,
and ask, "Will you be mine?"

HERE'S WHAT YOU NEED

Small clay pot

Pipe cleaners

Construction paper (red and pink)

Child safety scissors

Stapler

White craft glue

Thin strips of scrap paper

Play dough or clay

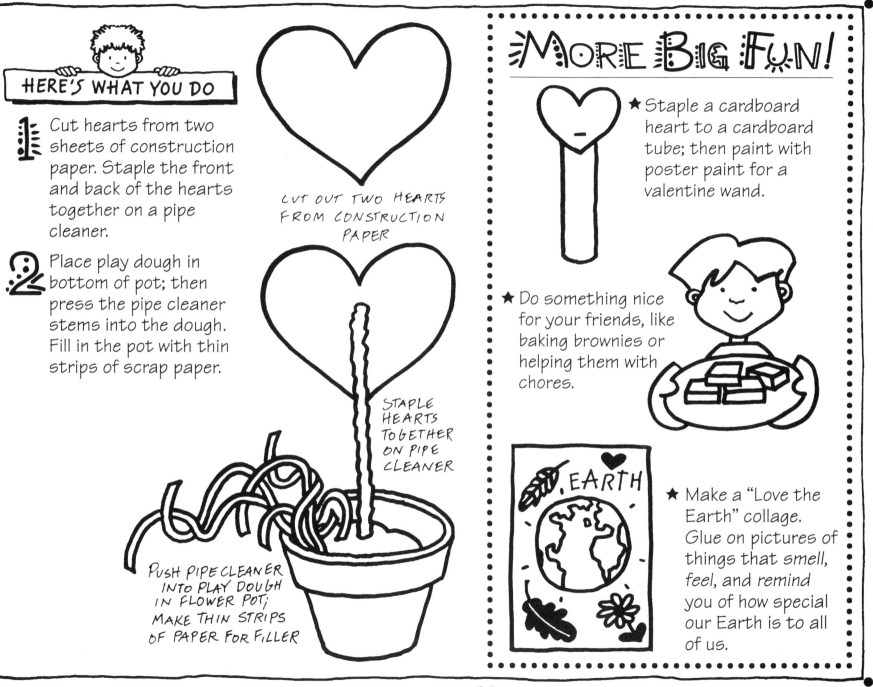

HERE'S WHAT YOU DO

1 Cut hearts from two sheets of construction paper. Staple the front and back of the hearts together on a pipe cleaner.

2 Place play dough in bottom of pot; then press the pipe cleaner stems into the dough. Fill in the pot with thin strips of scrap paper.

CUT OUT TWO HEARTS FROM CONSTRUCTION PAPER

STAPLE HEARTS TOGETHER ON PIPE CLEANER

PUSH PIPE CLEANER INTO PLAY DOUGH IN FLOWER POT; MAKE THIN STRIPS OF PAPER FOR FILLER

MORE BIG FUN!

★ Staple a cardboard heart to a cardboard tube; then paint with poster paint for a valentine wand.

★ Do something nice for your friends, like baking brownies or helping them with chores.

EARTH

★ Make a "Love the Earth" collage. Glue on pictures of things that *smell*, *feel*, and remind you of how special our Earth is to all of us.

TEA PARTY PLACE MAT

Gather your stuffed animals,
to keep you company,
And join them at the table,
for a party and tea!

HERE'S WHAT YOU NEED

Construction paper 9" x 12"
(22.5 cm x 30 cm)

Tissue paper

Child safety scissors

White craft glue

Clear contact paper

HERE'S WHAT YOU DO

 1 Tear tissue paper into shapes; then glue onto construction paper.

 2 Cut two sheets of clear contact paper 10" x 13" (25 cm x 32.5 cm). Place construction paper onto sticky side of one sheet; then press second sheet on top. Smooth out air bubbles and trim edges for a place mat.

3 Set a party table using the place mats; then invite your friends and their stuffed animals to tea.

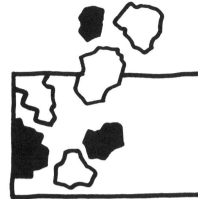

GLUE TORN TISSUE PAPER ON CONSTRUCTION PAPER

CONTACT PAPER

CONTACT PAPER

PLACE CONSTRUCTION PAPER BETWEEN STICKY SIDES OF TWO SHEETS OF CONTACT PAPER

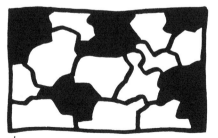

TRIM EDGES OF PLACE MATS

MAKE ENOUGH FOR COMPANY

MORE BIG FUN!

★ Have a tea party with a theme. Make leaf place mats in the fall and serve apple cider.

★ Make thin sandwiches using peanut butter, egg salad, tuna fish, or cucumbers. Use a cookie cutter to cut the sandwiches into shapes.

★ Wear costumes from old clothes, hats, jewelry, and gloves. Invite an older neighbor to join you or take the party to that person!

FRIENDSHIP BRACELETS

A best friend is someone you can tell secrets to, They laugh at all your jokes, and like being with you!

HERE'S WHAT YOU NEED

Paper towel tube

Tissue paper

Child safety scissors

Poster paint (white)

White craft glue

2 small paintbrushes

2 heavy paper plates

HERE'S WHAT YOU DO

1 Pour a small amount of glue into one plate; then add a few drops of water. Pour a small amount of white paint into the other plate. Cut two sections of cardboard tube 1.5" (3.5 cm) wide for bracelets.

2 Paint bracelets with white poster paint. Dry completely.

3 Cut designs from tissue paper; then use brush to glue paper onto bracelets. Let dry before wearing bracelets.

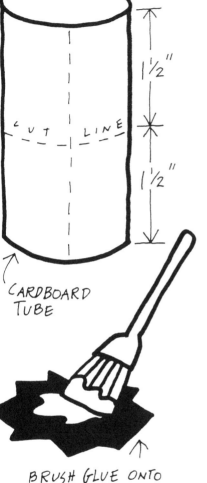

CUT LINE

1½"

1½"

CARDBOARD TUBE

BRUSH GLUE ONTO TISSUE PIECES; THEN PRESS PIECES ONTO CARDBOARD SECTIONS FOR BRACELETS.

MORE BIG FUN!

★ Take a picture with your friends; then glue four Popsicle sticks to fit around the photograph. Tape the photo to the back for a framed picture.

★ Read Frog and Toad Are Friends by Arnold Lobel.

★ Talk about how your friends make you feel. Are you happy when you are with them? Do they make you laugh?

BROWN BAG TURKEY

*Stuffed turkey in the oven,
good friends are on the way,
Mashed potatoes, pumpkin pie...
must be Thanksgiving Day!*

HERE'S WHAT YOU NEED

Brown lunch bag

Child safety scissors

Construction paper

Newspaper

White craft glue

Markers

Rubber band

HERE'S WHAT YOU DO

 Stuff the brown bag with sheets of crumpled newspaper. Trace a hand onto construction paper; then cut it out. Draw the head of a turkey with a long neck and waddle; then cut it out.

 Stick the neck of the turkey in the top of the bag; then wrap a rubber band around the neck of the bag.

3 Glue the paper hand onto the bottom of the bag for turkey feathers.

STICK NECK IN TOP OF BAG

STUFF A BROWN BAG WITH CRUMPLED NEWSPAPER

TRACE A HAND ON CONSTRUCTION PAPER

GLUE HAND ON BOTTOM OF BAG FOR TAIL FEATHERS

MORE BIG FUN!

★ Draw Thanksgiving Day pictures on a long sheet of shelf paper. Use as a table runner when you set the holiday table.

★ Ask everyone at dinner what they are most thankful for in this past year.

★ Make a turkey puppet. Trace outstretched hand on paper plate. Cut out and color (the thumb is the head; other fingers are feathers). Glue on Popsicle stick handle.

★ Cut out a large turkey from construction paper. Write a note on paper feathers about something you are thankful for. Glue them on the turkey, adding more feathers each year.

HAPPY NOTEPAPER

*Write a letter to some friends
who live far away,
Tell them everything that's new,
and brighten up their day!*

HERE'S WHAT YOU NEED

White stationery

Heavy paper plate

Plastic bottle cap

Poster paint

Markers (fine point)

1 Pour a small amount of poster paint in the plate. Dip the bottle cap into the paint; then press onto stationery for circles. Let dry.

2 Draw funny faces in the circles for happy notepaper.

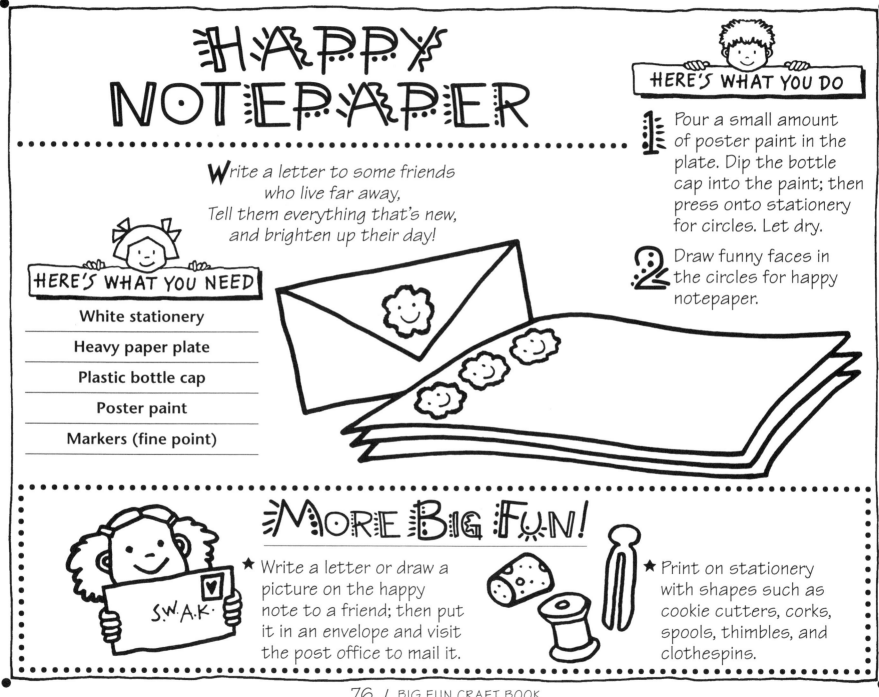

S.W.A.K.

MORE BIG FUN!

★ Write a letter or draw a picture on the happy note to a friend; then put it in an envelope and visit the post office to mail it.

★ Print on stationery with shapes such as cookie cutters, corks, spools, thimbles, and clothespins.

AROUND-THE-WORLD CELEBRATIONS

AMERICA: YANKEE DOODLE DANDY HEADBAND

You're invited to a party,
July fourth is the great day,
Flags will fly and people will sing,
"Happy Birthday, U.S.A.!"

HERE'S WHAT YOU NEED

Construction paper
(red, white, or blue)

White paper

Child safety scissors

White craft glue

Marker (red)

White chalk

Straws

Stapler

HERE'S WHAT YOU DO

1 Cut a band of red, white, or blue construction paper 4" (10 cm) wide. Cut length to fit around head; then fold over and staple together for a headband.

2 Cut white paper into four 3" x 4" (7.5 cm x 10 cm) rectangles. Cut blue paper into four 1" x 2" (2.5 cm x 5 cm) rectangles; then glue onto upper left corner of white paper for flags.

3 Use the red marker to draw stripes on the flag, and the white chalk to draw on stars. Staple flags onto straws; then staple straws inside fold of headband.

CUT A BAND OF CONSTRUCTION PAPER

FIT BAND AROUND HEAD, OVERLAP ENDS, AND STAPLE

BLUE

← STAPLE FLAG TO STRAW

RED

GLUE SMALL BLUE RECTANGLE ON FLAG SHAPE

DRAW RED STRIPES WITH MARKER

STAPLE STRAW TO INSIDE OF HEADBAND

MORE BIG FUN!

★ Bake a Fourth of July cake. Decorate it to look like a flag with white icing, rows of strawberries for stripes, and blueberries for stars.

★ March to the music of John Philip Sousa.

★ Learn to whistle "Yankee Doodle Went to Town." If you aren't a whistler, then hum it into a kazoo.

★ Talk about what it means to live in "the land of the free."

EGYPT: CRACKLED EGG ART

Shem al Neseem means "smell the breeze,"
Egyptians welcome spring;
With roses red and fancy clothes
and families picnicking!

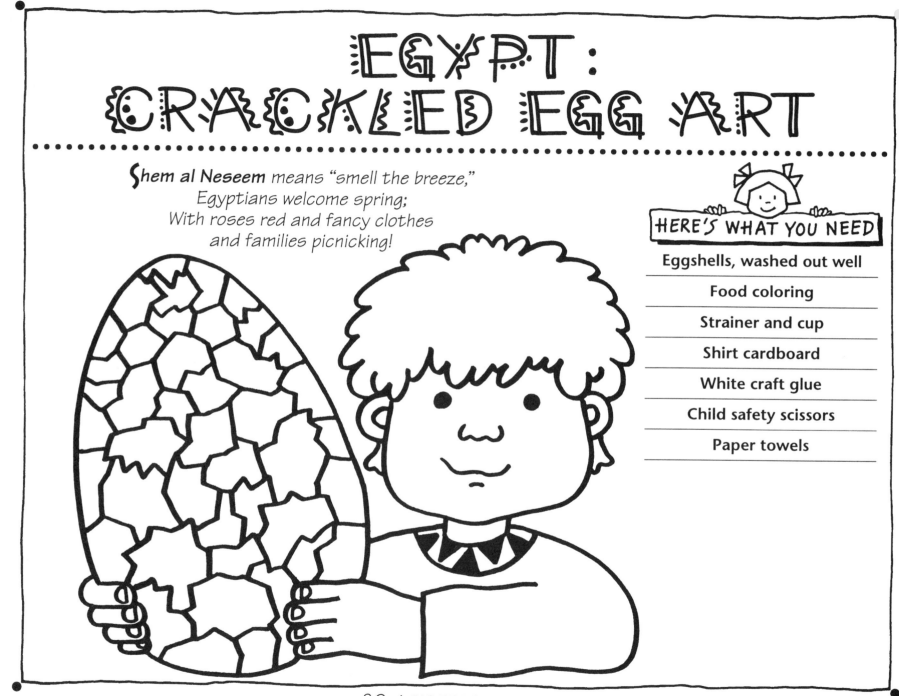

HERE'S WHAT YOU NEED

Eggshells, washed out well

Food coloring

Strainer and cup

Shirt cardboard

White craft glue

Child safety scissors

Paper towels

HERE'S WHAT YOU DO

1 Cut out an egg shape from the cardboard. Add water and a few drops of food coloring to a cup.

2 Break eggshells into small pieces; then place them in food coloring. Strain shells when colored. Gently dry on paper towels.

3 Cover the cardboard egg with glue; then press on eggshells.

DRAW AND CUT OUT CARDBOARD EGG

PUT EGGSHELL PIECES IN FOOD COLORING

COVER EGG-SHAPED CARDBOARD WITH GLUE; THEN APPLY COLORED SHELLS

MORE BIG FUN!

★ Egyptians celebrate spring with a picnic breakfast. You can have a breakfast picnic, too. Fill a basket with hard-cooked eggs, bread, fruit, and cheese.

★ Which other spring-time holidays use eggs in the celebration? If you guessed *Easter* and *Passover*, then you are right on track. Why do you think eggs are used in these celebrations? Where else do you see eggs in spring?

★ Find Egypt on a map or globe of the world. What continent is Egypt in? Is Egypt close or far away from where you live on the map?

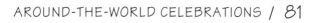

ISRAEL: SHOE BOX SUKKAH

The sukkah is a small hut with branches overhead, We celebrate the harvest, by eating fruit and bread!

HERE'S WHAT YOU NEED

Shoe box

Child safety scissors

Construction paper

String

Markers

HERE'S WHAT YOU DO

1 Ask a grown-up to help cut slits in the lid of the shoe box. Cut out one side of the box; then put the lid back on.

2 Cut construction paper into the shape of fruits and vegetables; then decorate with markers.

3 Use string to hang paper fruits and vegetables from the lid of the sukkah.

CUT OUT ONE SIDE OF BOX AND REPLACE LID

CUT OUT FRUITS AND VEGETABLES; THEN DECORATE

ATTACH STRING →

INSERT STRING THROUGH SLITS AND KNOT ENDS

MORE BIG FUN!

★ Sukkoth is a harvest celebration. Make a fruit or vegetable salad to celebrate your harvest season.

★ A sukkah is an outdoor hut, open to the sky, built to enjoy the harvest. Use a needle and thread to string popcorn; then hang it from the open roof of the sukkah.

★ Ask a grown-up to help you bake a *Challah*. It is the sweetened, braided bread eaten on the Jewish Sabbath and special holidays like Sukkoth.

★ Practice braiding with three pieces of heavy yarn. Once you get the method, you'll be ready to make a Challah.

JAPAN: STUFFED PAPER FISH

In Japan on **Children's Day**
family banners fly,
Along with streamers shaped like fish
from bamboo poles up high!

HERE'S WHAT YOU NEED

2 sheets of tissue paper

Used computer paper

Child safety scissors

White craft glue

Markers

HERE'S WHAT YOU DO

1 Cut a wide-mouthed fish from 2 sheets of tissue paper.

2 Squeeze a thin line of glue around the fish, (leave the mouth unglued); press the 2 sheets of tissue paper together.

3 Draw on fish's scales and eyes. Stuff the fish with torn computer paper and glue the mouth closed.

CUT OUT 2 FISH

GLUE FISH TOGETHER ALONG OUTER EDGES EXCEPT MOUTH

DRAW EYES, SCALES, AND OTHER DETAILS

STUFF FISH WITH TORN PAPER; THEN GLUE MOUTH

MORE BIG FUN!

★ Glue a pipe cleaner around the inside of the fish's mouth. Tie a long string through the fish for a kite.

★ Japanese children display their dolls for everyone to admire on Children's Day. Dress up your dolls or stuffed animals and show them to your friends.

★ Would you like to celebrate Children's Day where you live? Are there any special family days that seem like they are planned for children? Are special treats

CHINA: PAPER BAG DRAGON

Paper dragons lead the way,
the **Chinese New Year** has come,
Gung Hay Fat Choy means *"Good luck
and happiness everyone!"*

HERE'S WHAT YOU NEED

Large brown paper bag

Child safety scissors

Tissue paper

White craft glue

Poster paint

Paintbrush

Newspaper

HERE'S WHAT YOU DO

1 Cover table with newspaper. Cut the bag in half on a diagonal. Cut two nostril holes in the side of the bag. (Actually, you'll use these to see out.)

2 Glue long strips of tissue paper onto the bag for streamers; then paint on colorful designs. Let dry completely before wearing your dragon costume.

CUT FRONT OF BAG IN HALF AND SIDES ON A DIAGONAL

CUT OUT NOSTRIL HOLES (THESE ARE ACTUALLY THE EYE HOLES)

GLUE STREAMERS ON BACK; THEN ADD DECORATIONS

MORE BIG FUN!

★ Red is the Chinese color for happiness and good luck. Do you have a good luck charm or color?

★ What colors make you feel *happy*? What colors make you feel *sad*? What holidays do you celebrate that have special colors?

★ Read *Chin Chiang and the Dragon's Dance* by Ian Wallace.

NIGERIA: OATMEAL BOX DRUM

It's harvest in Nigeria;
let's dance and beat tin drums!
The **Zolla Festival** is held
as the great New Year comes!

HERE'S WHAT YOU NEED

Large, round oatmeal container (with top and bottom)

Child safety scissors

Finger paint

Glossy white paper (shelf paper)

White craft glue

Newspaper

HERE'S WHAT YOU DO

1 Cover the table with newspaper.

2 Cut shiny white paper to fit around the container. Finger paint designs on paper. Let dry completely.

3 Glue white paper around can for a drum.

CUT WHITE PAPER TO FIT AROUND CONTAINER

PAINT A DESIGN ON PAPER

GLUE PAPER AROUND CONTAINER

MORE BIG FUN!

★ Cover a cotton ball with a square of fabric. Hold it on the end of a pencil with a rubber band for a drumstick.

★ Ask a librarian to help you find some Nigerian or other African music. Listen to the drum beat and play along.

★ The Nigerians are proud of their harvest. Do you do anything special to celebrate the harvest, like have a corn-on-the-cob roast or eat cucumber and tomato sandwiches?

★ Read *La La Salama* by Hannah Bozylinsky.

INDIA: FLOATING DIWALI CANDLES

Far, far away in India
***Diwali** is the day,*
For wearing brightly colored clothes
while candles light the way!

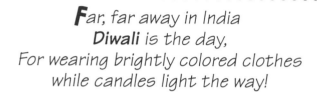

HERE'S WHAT YOU NEED

Heavy paper bowl

Toilet tissue tube

Recycled aluminum foil

White craft glue

Child safety scissors

Construction paper scraps
(red or orange)

HERE'S WHAT YOU DO

1. Cut the cardboard tube in half; then wrap it in aluminum foil.

2. Cut a flame from construction paper and glue it to the inside of the cardboard for a pretend candle.

3. Dip the bottom of the candle in glue, then place it in the center of the bowl. Float the bowl with the candle in water.

CUT TUBE IN HALF

WRAP IN FOIL

CUT OUT FLAME AND GLUE INSIDE TUBE

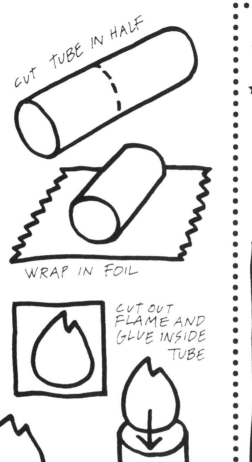

GLUE CANDLE IN BOWL

MORE BIG FUN!

★ In India, candles light the way for good luck in *Diwali*, or the New Year. How do you celebrate the New Year in your home? What things do you wish for?

JAN 1

★ The walls in the homes in India are decorated with designs made with white-rice flour water and filled in with color. Mix flour and water to make a runny paste; then add a few drops of food color. Put mixture into squeeze bottles and create designs on cardboard.

★ Candles are just one way people "light" their lives. Can you think of other things that make light? How about a flashlight? A lamp?

VIETNAM: SWINGING LANTERNS

*Bamboo poles are strung with charms,
the smell of food is near,
Everyone is all dressed up
for Tet, Vietnamese New Year!*

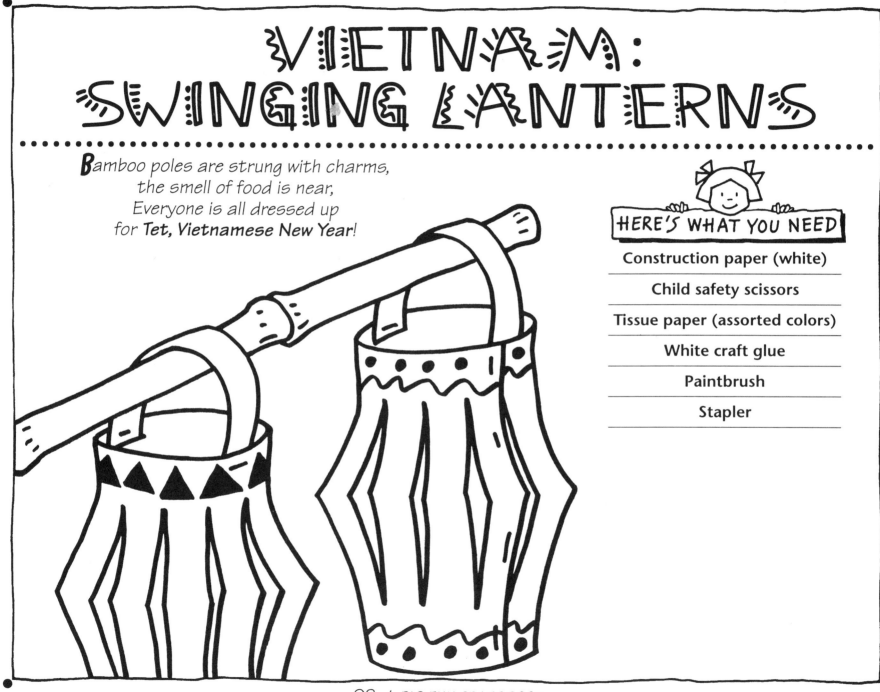

HERE'S WHAT YOU NEED

Construction paper (white)

Child safety scissors

Tissue paper (assorted colors)

White craft glue

Paintbrush

Stapler

HERE'S WHAT YOU DO

 Mix glue with a few drops of water. Use brush to glue small pieces of tissue paper onto construction paper. Let dry completely.

 Fold construction paper in half lengthwise. Cut slits 1" (2.5 cm) apart along the fold and stopping 1" (2.5 cm) below the edge of the paper.

3 Open the paper and staple together vertically for a lantern. Staple a strip of construction paper across the top of the lantern for a handle.

GLUE TISSUE PIECES ON CONSTRUCTION PAPER

FOLD PAPER IN HALF; THEN CUT 1" SLITS ALONG FOLDED EDGE

OPEN PAPER, STAPLE TOGETHER; THEN ADD HANDLE

⁂ MORE BIG FUN!

★ Cut a large circle from construction paper; then make a single cut from the outside edge of the circle into the center. Overlap edges of the circle; then staple together for a Vietnamese-styled hat.

★ In Vietnam, a favorite treat for the New Year is sweetened coconut. Is there a sweet treat you eat for a special holiday?

★ The sound of fire-crackers fills the air during the Vietnamese New Year. Bang a wooden spoon on the lid of a metal pot for a loud noise. Then tap gently for a *quiet* noise.

ENGLAND: PRESSED FLOWER CARD

Fill a basket with flowers today's the first of May! Then surprise special friends with blooms in their doorway!

HERE'S WHAT YOU NEED

Small flower

Clear contact paper

Construction paper

Child safety scissors

Tape

Markers, several colors

HERE'S WHAT YOU DO

1 Fold construction paper into fourths for a greeting card. Cut out a small opening in the front fold of the card.

2 Press the flower between two pieces of contact paper; then trim to fit behind the opening in the card.

3 Tape contact paper in place. Write colorful greetings inside the card.

FOLD PAPER INTO FOURTHS

CUT OUT

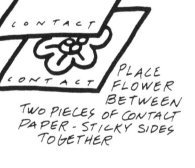

PLACE FLOWER BETWEEN TWO PIECES OF CONTACT PAPER - STICKY SIDES TOGETHER

TRIM AND TAPE IN PLACE

MORE BIG FUN!

★ Decorate a long cardboard wrapping paper tube with brightly colored tissue paper flowers and crepe paper streamers for a May pole.

★ Ask permission to pick some wildflowers. How many different colors can you find? Are some colors *bright* and others *dark*?

★ It's fun to press flowers between sheets of paper towels. Put heavy books on top and allow them to dry for a few days. Make a pressed flower bouquet by gluing an arrangement of flowers on a piece of heavy paper.

CANADA: SPONGE PRINT GIFT WRAP

Boxes wrapped in pretty paper,
great gifts to give away,
Today's December 26th,
*it must be **Boxing Day**!*

HERE'S WHAT YOU NEED

Roll of shelf paper or butcher paper

Sponge

Poster paint

Child safety scissors

Heavy paper plate

Newspaper

HERE'S WHAT YOU DO

 Cover the table with newspaper. Cut the sponge into a shape. Pour a small amount of paint into a heavy paper plate.

DRAW DESIGN SHAPE ON SPONGE AND CUT OUT

2 Dip the sponge in paint, then press onto paper for prints. Let dry completely. Use paper for gift wrap.

DIP SPONGE IN PAINT, THEN PRINT ON PAPER

MORE BIG FUN!

★ Print on paper with things such as bottle caps, cookie cutters, corks, and paper towel rolls.

★ Fill a long cardboard tube with small treats such as candy, toy cars, small balls, crayons, bubble bath, and a jump rope. Wrap the tube in sponge print paper for a gift.

★ Do you think it is more fun to *give* a gift or to *receive* a gift? What's your favorite gift you ever made for someone else?

ITALY: BERRY BASKET CRICKET HOUSE

Celebrate **Cricket Festival** in Florence, Italy, Carry your crickets in a house, and they'll chirp merrily!

HERE'S WHAT YOU NEED

2 plastic berry baskets

Twist ties

Shirt cardboard

Child safety scissors

Lettuce leaf and grass

HERE'S WHAT YOU DO

 Cut the cardboard to fit in the bottom of a berry basket.

 Lay cardboard, grass, and a lettuce leaf in the basket.

3 Turn the second basket upside down and attach with twist ties for a cricket house.

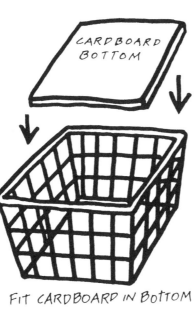

CARDBOARD BOTTOM

FIT CARDBOARD IN BOTTOM

ATTACH BASKETS TOGETHER WITH TWIST TIES

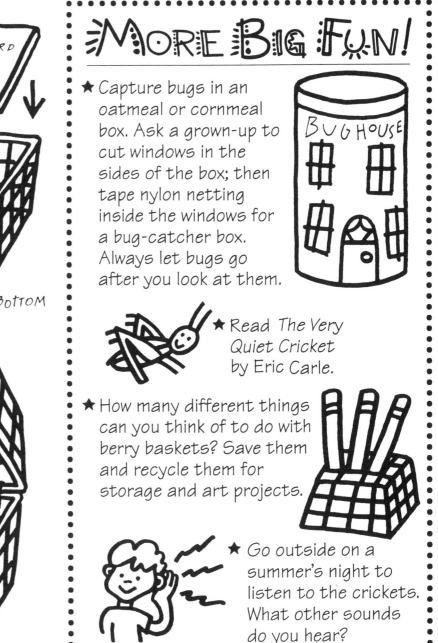

MORE BIG FUN!

★ Capture bugs in an oatmeal or cornmeal box. Ask a grown-up to cut windows in the sides of the box; then tape nylon netting inside the windows for a bug-catcher box. Always let bugs go after you look at them.

BUG HOUSE

★ Read *The Very Quiet Cricket* by Eric Carle.

★ How many different things can you think of to do with berry baskets? Save them and recycle them for storage and art projects.

★ Go outside on a summer's night to listen to the crickets. What other sounds do you hear?

MEXICO: SEED SHAKER MARACAS

At a Mexican *Fiesta* people celebrate all day, And gather in the evening for a fireworks display!

HERE'S WHAT YOU NEED

2 paper cups

Recycled aluminum foil

Masking tape

Dried beans or seeds

Child safety scissors

Tissue paper

White craft glue

HERE'S WHAT YOU DO

1 Place a few beans or seeds in one cup. Turn the second cup upside down on top of the first cup. Tape cups together for a maraca.

 Wrap the maraca in aluminum foil; then glue on tissue paper decorations.

PUT BEANS IN ONE CUP, TURN OTHER CUP UPSIDE DOWN ON TOP; THEN TAPE BOTH CUPS TOGETHER

WRAP IN FOIL AND GLUE ON COLORFUL DECORATIONS

MORE BIG FUN!

★ Listen to Mexican music, wear colorful clothes, and shake your maracas to the beat.

★ A piñata is made from papier-mache and is filled with small toys and treats. Children in Mexico wear a blindfold as they swing and try to break it open. What sweets do you eat at a festival or fair? Cotton candy? Caramel corn? Ice cream?

★ Find an old sombrero, put it on the floor, and dance around it with some friends. Ask a grown-up to teach you the Mexican Hat Dance.

BRAZIL: PEEK-A-BOO CARNIVAL MASK

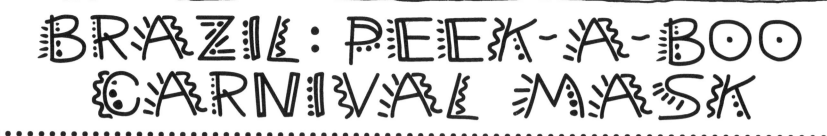

HERE'S WHAT YOU NEED

Large white paper plate

Poster paint

Paintbrushes

Yarn and string

Child safety scissors

White craft glue

Stapler

*C*ome to **Carnival** in Brazil!
parades are about to begin,
Everyone's singing and dancing
so please do join right in!

HERE'S WHAT YOU DO

1 Cover table with newspaper. Make a single cut from the outside edge of the paper plate into the center; then overlap edges and staple together to form a slight peak in the center.

2 Cut holes in the mask for eyes; then tie string on each side to hold mask in place.

3 Paint a face on the plate; then glue on yarn for hair.

MORE BIG FUN!

★ String packing popcorn with a needle and thread for a necklace to wear at your carnival celebration.

NEIGHBORHOOD

GHOSTLY SPONGE PRINTS

There's a way to make a friendly ghost,
this is what you can do,
Take a sponge and pour some paint,
the rest is up to you!

HERE'S WHAT YOU NEED

Sponge

Poster paint (white)

Heavy paper plate

Child safety scissors

Construction paper
(dark colors)

Marker (black)

Newspaper

DRAW A GHOST SHAPE ON A SPONGE AND CUT IT OUT

HERE'S WHAT YOU DO

1 Cover the table with newspaper; then pour a small amount of paint into the plate.

2 Cut a ghost shape from the sponge. Dip the sponge into paint; then press down onto paper for a ghost print. Use the marker to draw the ghost's eyes and mouth. Make lots of ghostly prints.

DIP SPONGE INTO PAINT AND PRINT ON PAPER

MORE BIG FUN!

★ If you carve a jack-o-lantern, save the pumpkin seeds. Wash them, dry them, and bake them in a 350°F oven with a grown-up's help. Yum!

★ Read Bony Legs by Joanna Cole.

PAPER BAG MAIL POUCH

The mail carrier brings letters, here's one from a friend: "There's going to be a party so please do attend!"

HERE'S WHAT YOU NEED

Large grocery bag

Child safety scissors

Stapler

Markers

HERE'S WHAT YOU DO

1. Cut a 6" (15 cm) strip from the top of the bag; then fold in the bag's edge.

2. Fold over the strip and staple it to the inside of the bag for a strap.

3. Decorate the mail pouch.

CUT STRIP FROM TOP OF BAG FOR STRAP

6"

FOLD IN TOP EDGE

FOLD OVER STRAP; THEN STAPLE TO BAG

MORE BIG FUN!

★ Did you ever get a letter in the mail? What did it say? Who was it from?

JAPAN
ITALY

★ Ask your friends and relatives to save unusual stamps for you. Sort the stamps by the country they are from, or by colors.

★ Cover a shoebox in recycled wrapping paper. Ask a grown-up to cut a slit in the top and use it for a mailbox.

MISS MARY

MAILBOX

★ Look in a World Atlas to see where your stamps are from.

PAPER PLATE STOP SIGN

On your way to school each day there's someone that you meet, The crossing guard tells you when it's safe to cross the street!

HERE'S WHAT YOU NEED

Large white paper plate

Construction paper (red)

White craft glue

Child safety scissors

Cardboard paper towel tube

Marker (black)

Stapler

HERE'S WHAT YOU DO

 Cut out an octagon (eight-sided shape) from the center of the plate; then trace the shape onto construction paper.

2. Cut out the construction paper and glue onto the plate.

3. Use black marker to write the word "STOP" on the sign.

4. Staple the octagon onto the towel tube for a STOP sign.

CUT OCTAGON SHAPE OUT OF PAPER PLATE, TRACE SHAPE ON RED PAPER, CUT OUT AND GLUE TOGETHER

STAPLE TUBE ON BOTTOM SIDE OF OCTAGON

MORE BIG FUN!

★ Draw a picture of children walking between the white chalk crossing lines to get to school.

★ Make up other signs. What might a sign look like that means "Don't Touch," or "Baby Sleeping"? Make some signs for your bedroom door.

★ Next time you're in the car, count how many STOP signs you see. Why do you think STOP signs are important to watch for?

FOIL MIRROR HEADBAND

A *pain, an ache, a bruise, a bump —
the doctor always knows
Exactly how to fix you up,
from your head to your toes!*

HERE'S WHAT YOU NEED

Shirt cardboard

Construction paper

Recycled aluminum foil

Child safety scissors

Stapler

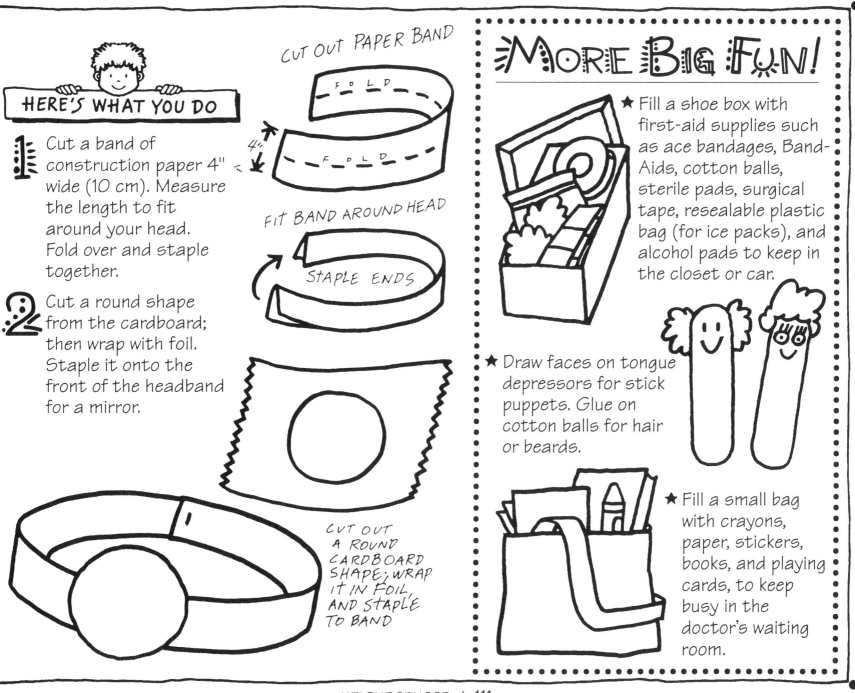

HERE'S WHAT YOU DO

1 Cut a band of construction paper 4" wide (10 cm). Measure the length to fit around your head. Fold over and staple together.

2 Cut a round shape from the cardboard; then wrap with foil. Staple it onto the front of the headband for a mirror.

CUT OUT PAPER BAND

FOLD

4"

FOLD

FIT BAND AROUND HEAD

STAPLE ENDS

CUT OUT A ROUND CARDBOARD SHAPE; WRAP IT IN FOIL, AND STAPLE TO BAND

MORE BIG FUN!

★ Fill a shoe box with first-aid supplies such as ace bandages, Band-Aids, cotton balls, sterile pads, surgical tape, resealable plastic bag (for ice packs), and alcohol pads to keep in the closet or car.

★ Draw faces on tongue depressors for stick puppets. Glue on cotton balls for hair or beards.

★ Fill a small bag with crayons, paper, stickers, books, and playing cards, to keep busy in the doctor's waiting room.

"OPEN WIDE" PAPER BAG PUPPET

HERE'S WHAT YOU NEED

Small brown paper bag

Construction paper (red and white)

White craft glue

Markers

Child safety scissors

Your dentist takes care of your teeth
to keep them sparkling white,
But you must also do your part,
and brush them every night!

HERE'S WHAT YOU DO

1 Draw the puppet's upper lip on the top flap of the bag; then draw the bottom lip on the bag just under the flap.

2 Cut the tongue and mouth from red construction paper; then glue them under the flap.

3 Cut out the puppet's eyes and teeth from white paper; then glue them onto the puppet.

MORE BIG FUN!

★ Use an egg timer to time yourself when you're brushing your teeth.

OUTDOOR FUN

CARDBOARD CARTON OBSTACLE COURSE

A *tricycle has three small wheels,*
bicycles have two,
Whichever one you chose to ride,
wear a helmet, too!

HERE'S WHAT YOU NEED

Large cardboard boxes

Poster paint

Large paintbrush

Heavy paper plate

Newspaper

HERE'S WHAT YOU DO

1 Cover the floor with newspaper. Pour a small amount of paint into the paper plate. Paint the cartons. Let dry completely.

2 Place boxes in an obstacle course formation; then ride bicycles around them.

MORE BIG FUN!

★ Paint cartons with traffic signs such as Railroad Crossing, Steep Hill, Curves In Road, and Deer Crossing.

STEEP HiLL

★ Decorate bikes with crepe paper streamers for a parade on wheels.

★ Everyone tell one safe-biking rule.

WEAR A HELMET!

FLASHLIGHT FUN

*Camping out can be great fun,
though you won't get much sleep —
Instead of telling stories,
you should be counting sheep!*

HERE'S WHAT YOU NEED

Flashlight

Paper cup

Pointed tool
(pencil point, nail, or pen)

HERE'S WHAT YOU DO

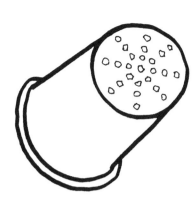

POKE HOLES IN
BOTTOM OF PAPER CUP

1 Carefully poke holes in a design on the bottom of the cup.

2 In a dark room or tent, shine the flashlight into the cup to see a pattern of light on the wall or ceiling.

3 Use additional cups to make different patterns. Turn cups to get a kaleidoscope effect.

PLACE CUP OVER LIGHTED FLASHLIGHT

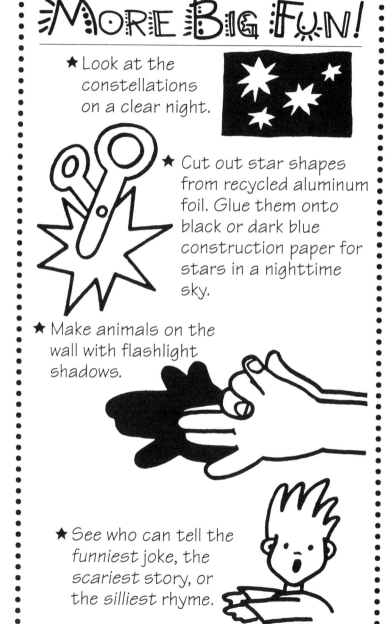

MORE BIG FUN!

★ Look at the constellations on a clear night.

★ Cut out star shapes from recycled aluminum foil. Glue them onto black or dark blue construction paper for stars in a nighttime sky.

★ Make animals on the wall with flashlight shadows.

★ See who can tell the funniest joke, the scariest story, or the silliest rhyme.

PICNIC PACKS

To plan the perfect picnic,
you'll need a sunny day,
Take a small picnic basket,
and games that you can play!

HERE'S WHAT YOU NEED

2 large cereal boxes

White or brown shelf paper or recycled gift wrap

Child safety scissors

Markers, several colors

Yarn

Tape

Stapler

HERE'S WHAT YOU DO

CUT OUT ONE SIDE (OPPOSITE SIDES) OF EACH BOX

1 Cut out one side panel from each cardboard box. Slide boxes halfway inside each other; then staple boxes together for a picnic pack.

2 Wrap boxes in shelf paper; then tape in place. Staple yarn onto sides of box for a strap.

3 Decorate the picnic pack. Store paper plates, cups, napkins, and utensils inside.

SLIDE ONE BOX INTO THE OTHER AND STAPLE

COVER PACK WITH SHELF PAPER AND TAPE

STAPLE ON YARN STRAP

MORE BIG FUN!

★ Press raisins into cream cheese or peanut butter spread in a stalk of celery for an "ants on a log" picnic snack.

★ Read Winter Picnic by Robert Welber.

★ What would you pack to eat and drink on a winter picnic? On a summer picnic?

EGG CARTON SEED STARTER

To start a little garden, plant a tiny seed, Give it water every day, and growth is guaranteed!

HERE'S WHAT YOU NEED

Egg carton

Planting soil

Seeds (flower or vegetable)

Popsicle sticks

Construction paper

White craft glue

Child safety scissors

Markers

LETTUCE TOMATO

HERE'S WHAT YOU DO

1 Fill each section of the egg carton half full with soil; then plant seeds.

2 Cut construction paper into 3" (7.5 cm) squares.

3 Draw on paper squares to identify the seeds. Glue paper onto Popsicle sticks.

4 Place sticks in soil. Place seed starter in a sunny window and water sparingly.

FILL EGG SECTIONS HALF FULL OF SOIL

PUSH SEEDS INTO SOIL

CUT SQUARE OUT OF PAPER; THEN GLUE ON POPSICLE STICK

RED RADISH

DECORATE FRONT OF CARD

MORE BIG FUN!

★ Transplant the seedlings from the egg carton to a larger container or the garden.

★ Visit a nearby farmer's market and see the different kinds of fruits and vegetables grown in your area.

★ Read *The Carrot Seed* by Ruth Krauss.

★ Look for tree seedlings before the lawn is mowed in the spring. Look for maple or elm tree seeds with bright green shoots close to the ground.

BUBBLE PRINTS

*It's fun to play in water,
by floating things on top,
Or blow bubbles with a straw,
and watch them go pop! pop!*

HERE'S WHAT YOU NEED

Large bowl

Liquid dishwashing detergent

Food coloring

Drinking straw

White paper

Newspapers

HERE'S WHAT YOU DO

1 Work outdoors or cover a table with newspaper. Pour 1/4 cup (50 ml) liquid dishwashing detergent into the bowl; then add a small amount of water and a few drops of food coloring.

2 Practice blowing out through a straw (don't suck in or you will get a mouthful of soap!). Blow into the bowl until bubbles rise to the top.

3 Gently lay a sheet of white paper over the bubbles for a colorful bubble print.

LAY WHITE PAPER OVER BUBBLES

BLOW INTO BOWL TO MAKE BUBBLES

← STRAW

MORE BIG FUN!

★ Fill a bucket with water and use a wide brush to "paint" outdoors. Watch as the drawing evaporates in the sun.

★ Shape pipe cleaners into wands. Mix together: 1/4 cup (50 ml) liquid dishwashing detergent, 3/4 cup (175 ml) cold water, and 5 drops glycerine (available at a pharmacy). Dip wand in bubble mixture and blow!

★ What colors do you see in the bubbles? Where else have you seen those colors?

RAINBOW SNOW

*Snow has fallen throughout the night,
to make a place to play,
Put on your mittens, scarf, and boots,
and then get out your sleigh!*

HERE'S WHAT YOU NEED

Bucket

Wide paintbrush

Food coloring

HERE'S WHAT YOU DO

1 Fill the bucket with water; then add a few drops of food coloring.

2 Use the brush to "paint" the snow.

MORE BIG FUN!

★ Look closely at freshly fallen snow. Do you see any animal tracks?

BIG FUN IN SPECIAL PLACES

THE ZOO: ZANY ZOO ANIMALS

*There's a place where people go
to see a kangaroo,
Lions, tigers, elephants,
all living at the zoo!*

HERE'S WHAT YOU NEED

Corrugated cardboard
(from carton)

Shirt cardboard

Poster paint

Paintbrush

Markers

Child safety scissors

Pencil

1 Draw on shirt cardboard the shape of zoo animals with 1/2" (1 cm) tabs extending from the legs. Cut out and draw on animals with markers. Paint the corrugated cardboard and let dry completely.

2 Ask a grown-up to cut small slits in the corrugated cardboard to fit tabs. Stand the animals upright in the slits.

CUT OUT ANIMAL SHAPE

DRAW DETAILS ON ANIMAL WITH MARKERS

INSERT TABS THROUGH SLITS IN CARDBOARD BASE

MORE BIG FUN!

★ Pick your favorite zoo animal; then *pretend* to act like it. Can anyone guess what you are?

★ Write each letter of the alphabet on twenty-four sheets of paper; then draw a picture of an animal (real or imaginary) whose name starts with that letter. Staple pages together for an *alphabet animal book*.

★ No zoo near you? Visit a pet store instead!

THE MUSEUM: FANCY FRAMES

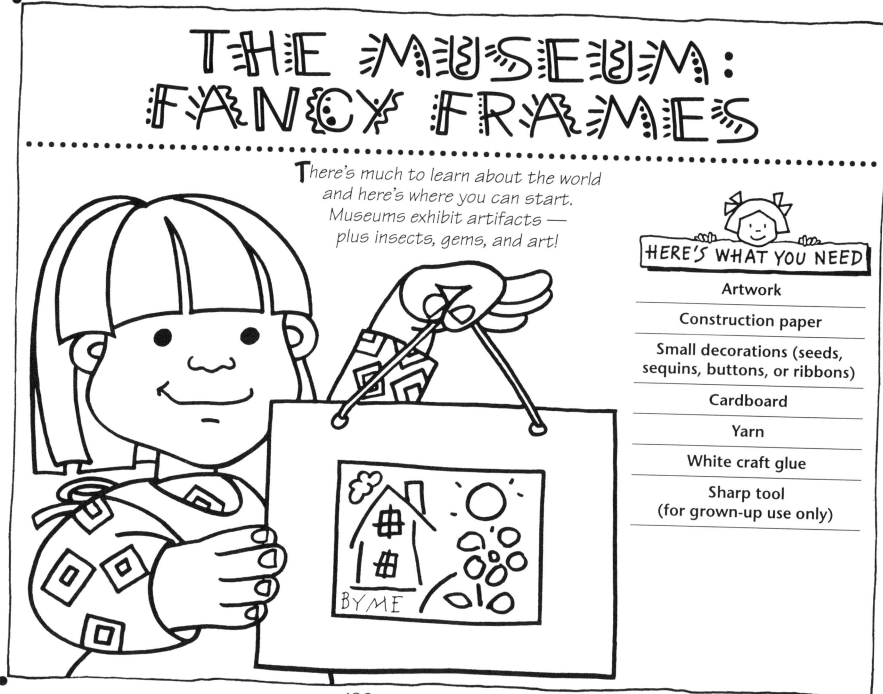

There's much to learn about the world
and here's where you can start.
Museums exhibit artifacts —
plus insects, gems, and art!

HERE'S WHAT YOU NEED

Artwork

Construction paper

Small decorations (seeds,
sequins, buttons, or ribbons)

Cardboard

Yarn

White craft glue

Sharp tool
(for grown-up use only)

BY ME

HERE'S WHAT YOU DO

1 Cut cardboard and construction paper 2" (5 cm) larger than the artwork.

2 Glue construction paper onto cardboard; then glue artwork in the center of the paper.

3 Glue small decorations around artwork; then make two holes in the top of the cardboard. Thread yarn through holes to hang artwork.

GLUE PAPER ONTO CARDBOARD

GLUE ARTWORK IN CENTER OF PAPER

BY ME

THREAD YARN THROUGH HOLES

GLUE SMALL DECORATIONS AROUND ARTWORK

BY ME

MORE BIG FUN!

★ Take a "Kids Like You Tour" at your local art museum. Find works of art that show children like you; then when you get home draw a self-portrait.

★ Do you like dolls or cars? Visit a doll museum or antique car museum.

★ What's your favorite picture? Is it a *painting* on the wall? A *photo* in a frame? A *drawing* in a book?

THE CIRCUS: STRAW ACROBATS

A circus clown is silly,
wearing such baggy clothes;
Those big feet make us giggle
as does a bright red nose!

HERE'S WHAT YOU NEED

Construction paper

Child safety scissors

Drinking straws

Pipe cleaners

Tape

Markers

HERE'S WHAT YOU DO

1 Draw the body of an acrobat on construction paper; then cut it out.

2 Tape pieces of pipe cleaner to the back of the acrobat for arms and legs. Draw acrobat's costume, face, and hair.

3 Bend pipe cleaner arms and wrap them around the straw for a trapeze.

DRAW AND CUT OUT BODY

TAPE PIPE CLEANERS TO BACK FOR ARMS AND LEGS

BEND AND WRAP PIPE CLEANER ARMS AROUND STRAW

DRAW COSTUME, FACE, AND HAIR

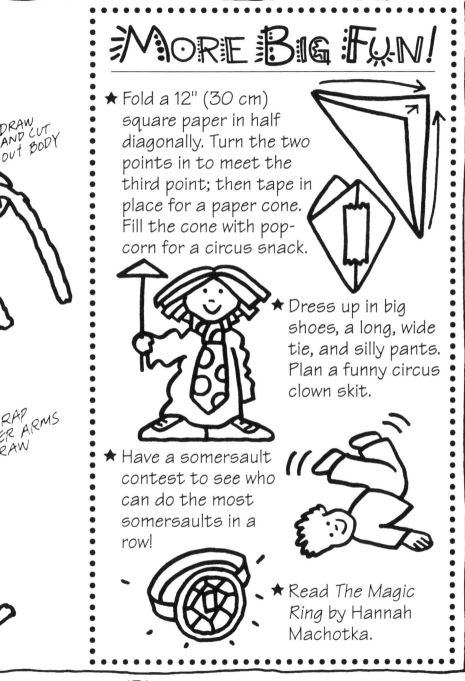

MORE BIG FUN!

★ Fold a 12" (30 cm) square paper in half diagonally. Turn the two points in to meet the third point; then tape in place for a paper cone. Fill the cone with popcorn for a circus snack.

★ Dress up in big shoes, a long, wide tie, and silly pants. Plan a funny circus clown skit.

★ Have a somersault contest to see who can do the most somersaults in a row!

★ Read *The Magic Ring* by Hannah Machotka.

THE BEACH: SEASHELL PAPERWEIGHT

*At the beach you'll play in sand,
along the ocean shore,
Then search for fancy seashells
there's so much to explore!*

HERE'S WHAT YOU NEED

Plaster of Paris

Seashells

Recycled margarine tub

Mixing stick

Poster paint

Paintbrush

Newspaper

STIR STICK

HERE'S WHAT YOU DO

1 Cover table with newspaper. Use stick to mix 1 cup (250 ml) Plaster of Paris with water until the consistency of paste. Pour plaster into the margarine tub.

2 Press shells in plaster and allow to harden completely.

3 Carefully remove plaster paperweight from tub. Decorate with poster paints or leave natural.

MIX PLASTER; POUR INTO MOLD

PRESS SHELLS INTO PLASTER

MORE BIG FUN!

★ Cover shirt cardboard with glue; then sprinkle on sand. Cut fish, sailboats, and a beach umbrella from construction paper; then glue onto cardboard for a beach scene.

★ Put a seashell to your ear. Can you hear the sound of the ocean?

★ At the beach, collect shells. Once home, sort unusual shells for a collection. Save the rest for art and craft projects.

★ Close your eyes and touch some different seashells. Do they feel smooth? Rough? Bumpy? Are they cool or warm?

THE LIBRARY: PHOTO BOOKMARK

*If you're looking for adventure,
the library is near,
A book can take you 'round the world,
without leaving your chair!*

HERE'S WHAT YOU NEED

Construction paper

Clear contact paper

Child safety scissors

Old snapshots

Hole punch

Yarn

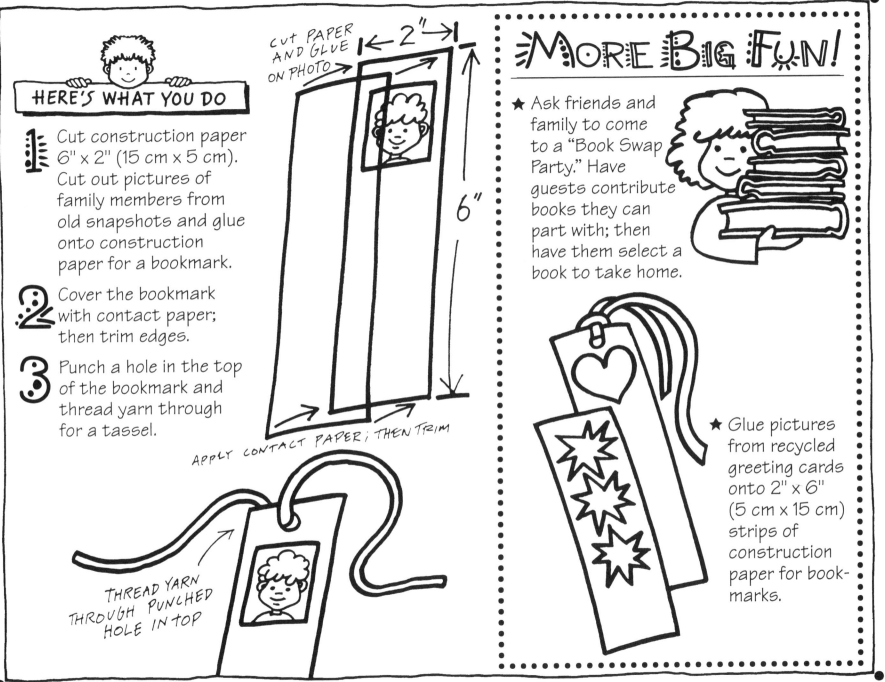

HERE'S WHAT YOU DO

1 Cut construction paper 6" x 2" (15 cm x 5 cm). Cut out pictures of family members from old snapshots and glue onto construction paper for a bookmark.

2 Cover the bookmark with contact paper; then trim edges.

3 Punch a hole in the top of the bookmark and thread yarn through for a tassel.

CUT PAPER AND GLUE ON PHOTO

2"

6"

APPLY CONTACT PAPER; THEN TRIM

THREAD YARN THROUGH PUNCHED HOLE IN TOP

MORE BIG FUN!

★ Ask friends and family to come to a "Book Swap Party." Have guests contribute books they can part with; then have them select a book to take home.

★ Glue pictures from recycled greeting cards onto 2" x 6" (5 cm x 15 cm) strips of construction paper for bookmarks.

THE FARM: OLD MACDONALD MURAL

*Farmers plow and plant and pick,
and some raise cattle, too,
They work all day from dawn to dusk
since there's so much to do!*

HERE'S WHAT YOU NEED

Roll of shelf paper or butcher paper

Child safety scissors

2 sponges

Poster paint (red and black)

2 heavy paper plates

Newspaper

Markers

HERE'S WHAT YOU DO

 1 Cover table with news-paper. Pour a small amount of red paint in a plate; then pour black paint into the other plate.

2 Cut one sponge in the shape of a triangle; then cut the other in the shape of a rectangle.

3 Dip the rectangular sponge into red paint; then press onto the roll of paper for the barn. Dip the triangular sponge in black paint for the roof on the barn.

 4 Draw things found on a farm, such as fences, pastures, trees, cows, pigs, gardens, or horses.

RED PAINT

BLACK PAINT

CUT OUT TRIANGLE

CUT OUT RECTANGLE

DIP TRIANGLE IN BLACK PAINT FOR ROOF

DIP RECTANGLE IN RED PAINT FOR BARN

MORE BIG FUN!

★ Fill a clean jar halfway with whipping cream. Tighten lid and shake jar six minutes for whipped cream; then continue shaking for butter.

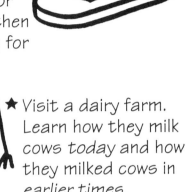

★ Visit a dairy farm. Learn how they milk cows *today* and how they milked cows in earlier times.

★ Would you like to live on a farm? What would be your favorite chore?

★ Read *Farmer Duck* by Martin Waddell.

THE AQUARIUM: PAPER PLATE FISH TANK

*When you go to aquariums
there're many fish to see,
The octopus, the sharks, the eel,
the whale and manatee!*

HERE'S WHAT YOU NEED

2 heavy paper plates

Plastic wrap

Recycled aluminum foil

Tape

Construction paper (blue)

Child safety scissors

Markers

HERE'S WHAT YOU DO

1 Cut out the center of one plate; then tape plastic wrap across the opening.

2 Trace plate center onto blue construction paper; then cut it out and glue it into the center of the second plate. Cut fish shapes from recycled aluminum foil and glue onto blue paper.

3 Decorate fish; then tape plates together for an aquarium.

DECORATE FISH AND GLUE ON BLUE PAPER; THEN GLUE PLATES TOGETHER

CUT OUT CENTER OF FIRST PLATE; THEN TAPE PLASTIC WRAP OVER OPENING

ON SECOND PLATE, GLUE BLUE PAPER CIRCLE IN CENTER

MORE BIG FUN!

★ Hang a string from a long pole and attach a magnet to the end of the string. Cut out fish from construction paper and put a paper clip on each one. Dangle the fishing line and try to "catch" a fish.

★ Visit an aquarium or a pet store. What is the main difference between fresh water fish and salt water fish?

★ Read *The Magic Fish* by Freya Littledale.

INDEX

LITTLE HANDS BOOKS

from Williamson Publishing

The following *Little Hands* books for ages 2 to 6 are each 144 pages, fully illustrated, trade paper, 10 x 8, $12.95 US. Please see last page for ordering information.

Children's Book-of-the-Month Main Selection
THE LITTLE HANDS ART BOOK
Exploring Arts & Crafts with 2- to 6-Year-Olds
by Judy Press

SHAPES, SIZES, & MORE SURPRISES!
A Little Hands Early Learning Book
by Mary Tomczyk

SUNNY DAYS & STARRY NIGHTS
A Little Hands Nature Book
by Nancy Fusco Castaldo—

The following *Kids Can!* books for ages 4 to 10 are each 160-178 pages, fully illustrated, trade paper, 11 x 8 1/2, $12.95 US.

THE KIDS' MULTICULTURAL COOKBOOK
Food & Fun Around the World
by Deanna F. Cook

KIDS' COMPUTER CREATIONS
Using Your Computer for Art & Craft Fun
by Carol Sabbeth

KIDS GARDEN!
The Anytime, Anyplace Guide to Sowing & Growing Fun
by Avery Hart and Paul Mantell

Winner of the Oppenheim Toy Portfolio Best Book Award!
American Bookseller Pick of the Lists
THE KIDS' SCIENCE BOOK
Creative Experiences for Hands-On Fun
by Robert Hirschfeld and Nancy White

Winner of the Parents' Choice Gold Award!
THE KIDS' MULTICULTURAL ART BOOK
Art & Craft Experiences from Around the World
by Alexandra M. Terzian

Winner of the Parents' Choice Gold Award!
Winner of Benjamin Franklin Best Juvenile Nonfiction Award!
KIDS MAKE MUSIC!
Clapping and Tapping from Bach to Rock
by Avery Hart and Paul Mantell

KIDS & WEEKENDS!
Creative Ways to Make Special Days
by Avery Hart and Paul Mantell

American Bookseller Pick of the Lists
KIDS' CRAZY CONCOCTIONS
50 Mysterious Mixtures for Art & Craft Fun
by Jill F. Hauser

Winner of the Oppenheim Toy Portfolio Best Book Award!
EcoArt!
Earth-Friendly Art & Craft Experiences for 3- to 9-Year-Olds
by Laurie Carlson

KIDS COOK!
Fabulous Food for the Whole Family
by Sarah Williamson and Zachary Williamson

THE KIDS' WILDLIFE BOOK
Exploring Animal Worlds through Indoor/Outdoor Crafts & Experiences
by Warner Shedd

HANDS AROUND THE WORLD
365 Creative Ways to Build Cultural Awareness & Global Respect
by Susan Milord

Winner of the Parents' Choice Gold Award!

THE KIDS' NATURE BOOK
365 Indoor/Outdoor Activities and Experiences
by Susan Milord

KIDS CREATE!
Art & Craft Experiences for 3- to 9-Year-Olds
by Laurie Carlson

Parents Magazine Parents' Pick

KIDS LEARN AMERICA!
Bringing Geography to Life with People, Places, & History
by Patricia Gordon and Reed C. Snow

American Bookseller Pick of the Lists

ADVENTURES IN ART
Art & Craft Experiences for 7- to 14-Year-Olds
by Susan Milord

MORE GOOD BOOKS FROM WILLIAMSON

Winner of Benjamin Franklin Best Juvenile Fiction Award!

TALES ALIVE!
Ten Multicultural Folktales with Activities
by Susan Milord
128 pages, full-color paintings and illustrations
Trade paper, $15.95

GREAT PARTIES FOR KIDS
35 Celebrations for Toddlers to Preteens
by Nancy Fyke, Lynn Nejam, Vicki Overstreet
128 pages, fully illustrated
Trade paper, $10.95

GROWING UP READING
Learning to Read through Creative Play
by Jill F. Hauser
144 pages, index
Trade paper, $12.95

SUGAR-FREE TODDLERS
Over 100 Recipes Plus Sugar Ratings for Store-Bought Products
by Susan Watson
176 pages, illustrated
Trade paper, $9.95

THE BROWN BAG COOKBOOK
Nutritious Portable Lunches for Kids and Grown-Ups
by Sara Sloan
192 pages, 150 recipes
Trade paper, $9.95

GOLDE'S HOMEMADE COOKIES
A Treasured Collection of Timeless Recipes
by Golde Hoffman Soloway
176 pages, over 130 recipes
Trade paper, $8.95

To Order:
At your favorite bookstore or order directly from Williamson Publishing. We accept Visa and MasterCard (please include number and expiration date), or send check to:

Williamson Publishing Company
Church Hill Road, P.O. Box 185
Charlotte, Vermont 05445

Toll-Free phone orders with credit cards:
1-800-234-8791

Please add $2.50 for first book plus 50¢ for each additional book. Satisfaction is guaranteed or full refund without questions or quibbles.

Prices may be slightly higher when purchased in Canada.